Prai

"Unlike any other publisher - happening in industry." – Pau... ..., ...Director, ... Sales, Fleet and Remarketing, Hyundai Motor America

"What C-Level executives read to keep their edge and make pivotal business decisions. Timeless classics for indispensable knowledge." – Richard Costello, Manager-Corporate Marketing Communication, General Electric

"Want to know what the real leaders are thinking about now? It's in here." – Carl Ledbetter, SVP & CTO, Novell Inc.

"Aspatore has tapped into a gold mine of knowledge and expertise ignored by other publishing houses." – Jack Barsky, Managing Director, Information Technology & Chief Information Officer, ConEdison *Solutions*

"Priceless wisdom from experts at applying technology in support of business objectives." – Frank Campagnoni, CTO, GE Global Exchange Services

"Aspatore publishes the answers to every business person's questions." – Al Cotton, Director, Nypro Corporate Image, Nypro Inc.

"Everything good books should be - honest, informative, inspiring, and incredibly well-written." – Patti D. Hill, President, BlabberMouth PR

"Answers questions that others don't even begin to ask." – Bart Stuck, Managing Director, Signal Lake LLC

"Unique insights into the way the experts think and the lessons they've learned from experience." – MT Rainey, Co-CEO, Young & Rubicam/Rainey Kelly Campbell Roalfe

"Must have information for business executives." – Alex Wilmerding, Principal, Boston Capital Ventures

"Reading about real-world strategies from real working people beats the typical business book hands down." – Andrew Ceccon, Chief Marketing Officer, OnlineBenefits Inc.

"Books of this publisher are syntheses of actual experiences of real-life, hands-on, front-line leaders--no academic or theoretical nonsense here. Comprehensive, tightly organized, yet nonetheless motivational!" – Lac V. Tran, Sr. Vice President, CIO and Associate Dean, Rush University Medical Center

"Aspatore is unlike other publishers...books feature cutting-edge information provided by top executives working on the front-line of an industry." – Debra Reisenthel, President and CEO, Novasys Medical Inc.

ASPATORE

www.Aspatore.com

Aspatore Books, a Thomson Reuters business, is the largest and most exclusive publisher of C-level executives (CEO, CFO, CTO, CMO, partner) from the world's most respected companies and law firms. Aspatore annually publishes a select group of C-level executives from the Global 1,000, top 250 law firms (partners and chairs), and other leading companies of all sizes. C-Level Business Intelligence™, as conceptualized and developed by Aspatore Books, provides professionals of all levels with proven business intelligence from industry insiders—direct and unfiltered insight from those who know it best— as opposed to third-party accounts offered by unknown authors and analysts. Aspatore Books is committed to publishing an innovative line of business and legal books, those which lay forth principles and offer insights that, when employed, can have a direct financial impact on the reader's business objectives, whatever they may be. In essence, Aspatore publishes critical tools—need-to-read as opposed to nice-to-read books—for all business professionals.

Inside the Minds

The critically acclaimed *Inside the Minds* series provides readers of all levels with proven business intelligence from C-level executives (CEO, CFO, CTO, CMO, partner) from the world's most respected companies. Each chapter is comparable to a white paper or essay and is a future-oriented look at where an industry/profession/topic is heading and the most important issues for future success. Each author has been selected based upon their experience and C-level standing within the professional community. *Inside the Minds* was conceived in order to give readers actual insights into the leading minds of business executives worldwide. Because so few books or other publications are actually written by executives in industry, *Inside the Minds* presents an unprecedented look at various industries and professions never before available.

Implementing a Successful HR Strategy

*Leading HR Executives on Attracting Talent,
Establishing Company Culture,
and Inspiring Employees*

ASPATORE

Mat #40796367

BOOK & ARTICLE IDEA SUBMISSIONS

If you are a C-Level executive, senior lawyer, or venture capitalist interested in submitting a book or article idea to the Aspatore editorial board for review, please e-mail TLR.Aspatore.Authors@thomson.com. Aspatore is especially looking for highly specific ideas that would have a direct financial impact on behalf of a reader. Completed publications can range from 2 to 2,000 pages. Include your book/article idea, biography, and any additional pertinent information.

Inside the Minds Project Manager, Kristen Skarupa; edited by Eddie Fournier; proofread by Melanie Zimmerman

ISBN 978-0-314-20296-3

For corrections, updates, comments or any other inquiries please e-mail TLR.AspatoreEditorial@thomson.com.

First Printing, 2008
10 9 8 7 6 5 4 3 2 1

CONTENTS

Working Together to Serve the Greater Good of the Company

Mark Fogel

Vice President, Human Resources and Administration;
Chief Human Resources Officer
Leviton

ASPATORE

Setting the Stage

Leviton Manufacturing was founded in 1906 as a manufacturer of gas mantle tips for gas lights. From humble beginnings, it has grown in stature, moving from gas to electrical applications and emerging as a leader in the electrical product industry more than one hundred years later. The company is broad and comprehensive in its approach to the marketplace, providing products for residential, commercial, and industrial use with more than 22,000 active SKUs (stock-keeping units). The company provides solutions from basic outlets, lighting controls, and GFCIs (ground fault circuit interrupters) to complete solutions for energy management, data centers, networking solutions, and more.

It has taken one hundred-plus years to reach this level of business prominence; however, it has been in only about the past eight years that the HR (human resources) function has taken shape and moved from an old-style "personnel department" to a fully functioning strategic partner to the business.

Establishing a Fresh Start

Prior to 2000, I would categorize our human resources function as traditional and administratively oriented. We did the normal hiring, benefits administration, and processing that goes with HR functions, both big and small, at most companies in the United States. We were solid but unspectacular in our service and lacking in bench strength of strategically oriented executives.

Our emergence to a strategic function occurred in two phases. The first, from 2000 to 2003, was our foundation-building period. We needed to do two things: hire a team that could get us from administrative to strategic and do a full court press by relentlessly building relationships, respect, programs, and processes. Each held extreme challenges. How do you attract top-level HR talent with little to offer but the hopeful opportunity to build something from scratch? To many this was too daunting a task, but to a few it was the challenge of a lifetime—especially to my two most senior business partners today, who team with me to drive the Leviton HR ship. My team, which is almost entirely intact from my first eighteen months with the company, all saw the possibilities and were critical to accomplishing everything we have done. The second task was as difficult in that we had minimal respect and were rarely engaged by management or staff for little more than a benefits question or assistance in making a hire.

So our sole strategic mission, once the team was assembled, was to re-engage the entire workforce and make HR relevant to them. We attacked this in numerous ways. We ran lunch-and-learns and after-work programs on a multitude of topics, some work-related, some health-related, and some life-related. We needed to find common connections to have dialogue. We also visited employees on their turf, popping up in offices, sitting with them in the lunchroom, and taking every opportunity to connect. We realized if they weren't coming to us, we needed to go to them. Eventually some of the workforce stopped seeing us as the enemy. We were even able to get invitations to occasional meetings to present information in a more formal setting. Occasionally we were able to offer a strategic idea or concept, and our senior management team was starting to loosen up and invite us in, as well.

After two years of working our plan, we were finally seeing the level of employee engagement that most HR teams take for granted. By the third year, we had broken through and were functioning with full employee buy-in to our baseline services. I truly believe that engagement is built on both likeability and mutual respect. We had found a good measure of both.

It was time to move to phase two. By the beginning of 2003, we were building off our newfound relationships and began to build and improve our programs and services. We also focused on processes (or lack thereof) and centralization of our corporate benefits and performance management—two areas that had been handled at a local level by business general management. This was a difficult challenge in that we were taking away responsibility and, in some eyes, the power associated with these two critical areas of human resources. My director of compensation and benefits brought a deep and thorough knowledge of benefit plan design to the table. My director of HR, responsible for talent management and development, did the same with performance management.

We had many conversations, presentations, and disagreements, but eventually we were able to wrest control away from the line. This was a demarcation point in our HR evolution, as this was the first time we had control of substantive functions and financial responsibility. With these big changes, small changes came easier, and momentum was starting to build. Small victories and a few large ones brought awareness that we could contribute at a much higher level. The executive management team expanded its outreach to my team and me to provide more complex services and programs. The word "strategic" was starting to replace "administrative." I was attending executive meetings and getting to voice an HR perspective to business issues. The stage was set to change the paradigm and make a leap to a whole new level of participation, one that was business-oriented. This occurred with two critical leadership changes at the end of 2005 and the beginning of 2006.

In the fall of 2005 our CEO, Harold Leviton, stepped aside from day-to-day responsibilities and appointed Don Hendler, our current president and CEO, into his role. We also promoted a senior vice president into our first chief operating officer position in January 2006.

We were at a point where our business had become mature and needed to be invigorated, and human resources was positioned with this new leadership group to truly be a partner and to help the company align its business processes and its business goals. We went from being somewhat of a servant relationship—in which we took orders and responded to tasks— to one in which we were truly partners and had a space at meetings to have the conversations well beyond the proverbial seat at the table. We were part of the conversation, and we were looked to for thought leadership and ideas and, more importantly, action as a result.

The one thing that changed for us, which really leads into a culture change in the company in responding to staff/employee satisfaction and staff output, was that we worked jointly with the senior leadership team and developed our management by objective (MBO) program, which takes into account five areas that our entire corporation is responsible to focus on each year.

Currently, the five MBOs that our corporation looks to are revenue growth, employee development, process improvement, innovation in product, and cost containment in everything that we do. This involves looking for avenues of cost containment or cost reduction. As a manufacturer, cost reduction is a critical aspect of our business and how we operate.

Working with Company Executives

We state to our executives across the enterprise that, if you are working on something that does not fit into one of these five areas, you are not working on it as a project, because it needs to align to what the company needs to do to grow, to be successful, and to return a higher level of profitability.

Human resources worked closely with our top one hundred executives who were responsible to update these objectives on a quarterly basis, and to the extent where we actually sat down with the leadership group to review what they were doing. We then sat down with our COO and reviewed the status of these objectives.

In essence, human resources knows everything that is going on in the whole corporation through updates on a quarterly basis, just by being involved in this process, and that is an amazing tool to have in human resources. Our role now shifted away from an administrative task orientation to addressing the things that these top one hundred executives need from us to support them in being successful and accomplishing these goals.

We are about a year-and-a-half into this process. We started it more than two years ago, but I would say it was a year-and-a-half ago when we really became involved. We get into granular conversations to a point where much of what we do strategically is an outgrowth of what comes up in these quarterly MBO alignment conversations. I think that is an important thing to know as a precursor to developing the right programs and services.

Business Transformation Leads to Culture Change

Before 2006, our culture could best be described as paternalistic. Our employees looked forward to lifelong employment. Even as our industry and others moved away from this in the late 1980s and 1990s, we maintained a strong culture best categorized by loyalty, patronage, and trust. We had created and maintained a home away from home, where every employee felt a level of security as a Leviton employee. Productivity and results were important, but relationships always came first. Family emergencies—health or otherwise—were given priority and assistance, even occasionally involving the owners of the company who were known to make calls to doctors and even reach into their pockets for a personal loan to help an employee through a hardship.

To the outside business community we were envied for our relationship-driven culture, which even extended to our vendors and customers. As we entered the new millennium, our company was starting to show some wear and tear from our cultural focus. Our competitors were becoming aggressive in innovation, efficiency, and pricing. Our culture was starting to become a barrier to competing and was in some ways showing stress fractures, as we were not focused on results, speed, and innovation. We had the capabilities, but we needed to adjust the culture to set these capabilities free to flourish.

As we passed the baton of leadership in 2006, we were also positioned to change the culture. Our new leadership required the company to be more disciplined in its approach to business, asking employees to focus, perform, and be accountable. This may have been the norm for most companies, but it was new for us. Transforming business practices was a big leap forward for us. Transforming a culture was exponentially more difficult. The vast majority of our employees had long tenure and were deeply rooted in our old culture. Many questioned our new business model and were confused by this dramatic change accomplished in a short window of time. Some just did not get it at all. A common comment was, "This is a different company than it has been the past twenty years. We have always done well. Why change now?"

The world had changed around us, and we had not. As an HR team, we were faced with how we were going to evolve the culture without losing some of the family elements that our employees yearned for. Just as every child grows up, we felt that we needed to stop treating our employees as their parents and start treating them with respect as adults in a family relationship. Instead of taking care of them, we need to provide education and services to allow them to make decisions about benefits and company services. This took shape in a few ways.

First, wellness has become part of our new culture. We share the responsibility by offering programs and opportunities to join other employees in active programs, from Weight Watchers to walk-at-lunch programs, discounted gym memberships, and health awareness presentations.

Second, we recognized being competitive required new and different skill sets. We now provide 100 percent reimbursement for college tuition programs, along with a robust development and training program, from leadership courses to voluntary project opportunities. The true responsibility to take advantage of the programs and services was placed on the employees; we simply provided outlets.

Third, we have become socially responsible in our communities. Every location in the company partners with its community. A great example is happening at our western distribution center in Reno, Nevada, where we have mentally challenged adults who come into our workplace to work on a joint-funded program with the community and are able to contribute and work. To be in Reno and see this group working each day and doing something that adds value to our business is not just good for these individuals and the community, but also it is good for our employees.

Here in our corporate offices, we did a project this summer with an organization called Long Island Volunteers. The group is similar in tone to Habitat for Humanity, but this organization asks local companies to choose a project and to have their employees come together and work on a project that usually takes only one or two days.

The key in all these changes is that it serves a purpose to help maintain some of our old culture as we forge ahead with a new culture. These changes fit together nicely as we try to transform our business to one of action and accountability, and HR plays a part on both ends of the equation.

Company Evolution: Implementing Successful Strategies

One of the things we have implemented is a scorecard that we use internally in HR. It is still a work in progress, but we measure everything. When you work, you want to be able to measure what you do, so we do measure what we do, and we benchmark against industry. In most categories, we do exceptionally well. Much of our success has to do with communication. One of the things that have been important for us in implementing HR strategies here is employee communication and using every vehicle we have to communicate.

We have people who work on computers all day, but we also have factories and distribution centers where the majority of our employees are hourly, work on a shop floor, and do not have regular access to a PC where they can receive an e-mail or see an intranet posting.

We have spent a great deal of time as we have rolled out our strategies in employee communication. I do not think you can ever over-communicate when it comes to that. I think that whether it is payroll attachments, e-mail blasts, putting an announcement up on a bulletin board, holding meetings at local facilities to talk about these things, or making communication part of staff meetings at a granular level—all of these types of communication are important in building a successful HR strategy.

Implementing a New HR Strategy

It is important to stay up-to-date with the outside business community. I put strong emphasis on this with my team to keep up-to-date with what others are doing that's new or different. My senior management team in HR is very involved in HR organizations, and we work closely with our third-party vendors, who help educate us. Our health care and compensation vendors, whom we look at as business partners, help educate us and keep us on the leading edge of what is going on in the HR community.

I ask my staff to attend regular conferences and monthly meetings at the different associations, and to attend legal briefings and other types of briefings as HR has become extremely regulatory with government and agency involvement. It is important that we always know what is going on and can make adjustments. When it comes to research, I think that we deal on a real-time basis with trying to stay current or trying to stay ahead of the curve about what is happening in the external environment. We then bring it in and apply it in a business sense.

I also ask my senior team to speak at conferences and participate in HR organizations actively. Taking a leadership role in the HR community offers the opportunity to give back and to round out their personal and professional experiences.

Technology as Part of Our HR Strategies

We have hit the age of Web 2.0. We were at the forefront of using intranet technology over the past nine years. Since I came to Leviton, we have expanded greatly on our use of electronic processes, both in HR and across the organization—not just from the standpoint of communicating, but also as a vehicle to connect people on projects and services, electronic forms, and things of that nature. Where we are going today is interesting. We have started to use Wikis on a corporate level. We are rolling them out in some of our line functions. Our human resources group has started a project on which we are about a month into using this technology.

It is brand new for us to be using Wikis. We can take some of the communication that clogs e-mail offline and do it in a more protected and collaborative environment. We are spending a lot of time on the recruiting front, working with social networks in recruiting staff or networking with other people who are doing similar types of work.

Our recruiters are on Craigslist; they're on LinkedIn; they're on Facebook; they're on these sites actively recruiting and connecting with people. It is a different age, and it is a virtual world we live in, and it is incumbent upon us to work with the cutting-edge technology—in HR and our organization—that Generation X and Generation Y are familiar with.

Budgeting to Implement HR Strategies

I can tell you that strategic projects are a small portion of our budget—probably less than 15 percent. With a small, lean staff, a majority of what we do each day goes into paying my staff and supporting things like our software infrastructure so that we have good data management. I do not think it is really about the money, because I could turn around and argue that in reality 90 percent of our budget goes into strategy, because every dollar I pay to my management team here in New York is with the goal of getting the strategic agenda done. We have to get tactical work done, but our value-add is to move this agenda forward.

It is difficult to put ROI (return on investment) to what we are doing. It depends on the perspective from which you look at it. I like the view that the majority of every dollar we spend in HR is focused on strategic return to the organization, or, in better terms, value-added return to the organization.

What's Next: Blurring the Lines between HR and the Business

The old paradigm was for HR to consult and coach. We were viewed as the "people resource." In the future, I believe successful HR functions need to be embedded inside the business instead of sitting outside at the fringes. Today we are moving to the center. My HR team goes to business staff meetings and participates on equal footing with product management, engineering, and marketing. I attend our executive meetings and have the ability to comment on not only people issues, but also business issues.

Talent management, performance management, and counseling are no longer the responsibility of the HR function. They are shared, and we help our executives carry out these duties by training and nurturing them in these areas.

Sustainability and the Greening of Business

The new workforce—especially Gen-Ys—has a renewed vigor to make sure we take care of the environment. This is the "wild, wild West" for business. Everyone seems to be jumping on the bandwagon, and yet we still know so little about what is best.

Concern for the environment needs to be more than the flavor of the day—it needs some structure and oversight. I think HR has a great opportunity to play a significant role in this area. I believe it will become an extension of employee benefits, but instead of a company taking care of employees and their families, it will care for their entire living and working environment. Consider it health management and wellness for their communities.

16

I believe the future is bright for the HR profession. We are positioned as professionals to be real value-added contributors to our businesses. We can align corporate agendas with the needs of our employees and create great outcomes if done right.

Mark Fogel is vice president, human resources and administration for Leviton Manufacturing Co. Inc. As the chief human resources officer, he has oversight for both corporate and regional facilities, supporting a population exceeding 10,000 employees in North America, Asia, and the Middle East.

The Society for Human Resource Management (SHRM) has named Mr. Fogel the Human Capital Business Leader of the Year for 2007, an award that goes to a senior HR professional who serves as a leading force in executing organizational strategy that directly affects the organization's performance and prominence. During his tenure at Leviton, Mr. Fogel has earned a reputation as a "get-it-done" executive who has re-engineered the HR function from an administrative body to a strategic business partner.

Mr. Fogel earned a master's degree from Adelphi University and a Bachelor of Arts degree from State University of New York at New Paltz.

Planning, Measuring, and Reporting the Business Case for Diversity

Georgia Coffey, M.Ed.

Director, Office of Equal Employment Opportunity and Diversity Management

U.S. Food and Drug Administration

ASPATORE

Adapting to a Rapidly Changing Marketplace

In this age of burgeoning globalization, never has it been more critical that organizations be able to adapt to a rapidly changing marketplace. Technology has obliterated economic and geographic boundaries. The private and public sectors will be competing in the same expanding consumer and labor markets. While companies will compete for market share, agencies will compete for the same high-quality, diverse human capital to service our new global community. The survival of organizations in the twenty-first century will depend largely on their ability to adapt to an increasingly diversified market and strategically manage their human resources accordingly.

Today's American workplace is a confluence of contradictions: old vs. new guard, generations X vs. Y, parochial vs. global perspectives, individual vs. team paradigms, hierarchical vs. flattening structures, homogeneity vs. infinite diversity. These seemingly conflicting dynamics pose a vexing challenge for today's leaders and human resources professionals: how do we manage these sometimes competing elements in a way that supports rather than impedes our mission?

Draconian shifts in our customer base will require significant changes in the human resources that service it. This portends opportunities as well as challenges for those of us in the human resources (HR) and equal employment opportunity and diversity management (EEO) arenas. As a director of EEO and diversity management for the U.S. Food and Drug Administration (FDA), I am acutely aware of the responsibilities public service leaders face in our increasingly global community. Today's workplace, like our marketplace, is no longer defined by a singular dominant profile. It is an amalgam of *what was, what is,* and *what is on the horizon.*

Our labor force, like our nation, is more diverse than ever in terms of race, color, gender, sexual orientation, ethnicity, religion, age, and disability status. New entrants into our civilian labor force are overwhelmingly diverse—characterized largely as foreign-born, people of color, and non-traditional workers. The American worker's profile is being redrawn. By most estimates, by 2040, we will no longer be a nation of any single demographic majority. This offers great opportunities for the public and private sectors, if we manage it effectively.

Break the Mold

Historically, organizations have met change by attempting to retrofit emerging differences into the dominant culture. New entrants into the labor force were expected to adopt the ways of the host organization. Not surprisingly, this approach was met with resistance and conflict in the workplace that were often counterproductive. Today, industries understand that to remain healthy and competitive, they must tap into the diverse spectrum of talent available and empower it, not suppress it. They must recruit diverse intellectual capital and cultivate a work environment that leverages differences. Diversity management will be a seminal strategy in achieving this.

In response to changing demographics in the workplace, companies offered cross-cultural communications training in a well-meant effort to pre-empt conflict. However, all too often these efforts served only to further compartmentalize cultures, while insisting on assimilation into the "corporate melting pot." Today, effective diversity management means managing our human resources and organizational culture in a way that allows for synergy and constructive conflict. It means enabling differences to thrive in order to reap the benefits of diverse perspectives. It also means cultivating a safe and open environment that encourages *divergent* rather than *convergent* thinking to achieve the best performance outcomes.

The public sector in particular must be wary of the dangers of "group think," often the result of a homogenized workforce and an insistence on maintaining the status quo. The propensity to perpetuate the status quo is pervasive in the public sector and difficult to overcome. However, insistence on the status quo is a harbinger of obsolescence at best, and a precursor to disaster at worst. We have all witnessed the tragic outcomes of rigid organizational cultures in both the public and the private sectors. The Columbia Shuttle tragedy was one such event where the failure was attributed in part to an organizational culture that squelched dissent and stifled differences of opinions.[1] To its great credit, NASA has responded with one of the strongest diversity management programs in federal service. Stovepipe cultures in the intelligence community also led to catastrophic failures in recent history, as revealed in the after-action reviews of 9/11.[2] Similarly, the private sector is not immune to the dangers of insular organizational cultures, as evidenced by the demise of Enron and WorldCom. Here again, corporate cultures were so isolated and impenetrable that their leaders believed they were above the rules and exempt from accountability. The results were calamitous for entire sectors of our economy.

Changing institutionalized cultures will not happen overnight. It will require transformative rethinking of our corporate mentality and the concomitant redesign of our organizational architecture. Companies and agencies will have to deconstruct silos, flatten ivory towers, and eliminate processes that lead to tunnel vision. Last but not least, it will demand shattering the vestiges of all barriers to equal opportunity and constructing models of participative leadership. This begins with a values-based vision and is implemented through deliberate, purposeful planning.

Strategic Planning

In the public sector, proactively managing change is a staple of the most successful agencies. Smart organizations know that unmanaged change is chaos, and missions without proper planning are rarely achieved. In the FDA, we have taken deliberate steps to draw a roadmap that guides us in our life-critical mission of *protecting and promoting the public health*. The FDA's strategic plan is a goal-driven framework designed to address emerging issues and evolving global demands in the area of food, drug, biologics, cosmetics, and medical device safety regulation. The FDA's ubiquitous imprint on the public health demands a proactive and aggressive plan that recognizes the importance of employing diverse scientific expertise that reflects the needs of the pluralistic society we serve.

---

[1] *Report of the Columbia Accident Investigation Board* (NASA, March 2003).
[2] *Report of the Commission on the Intelligence Capabilities Regarding Weapons of Mass Destruction* (February 2004).

In the area of workplace culture, the FDA is committed to creating a values-driven, science-led organizational culture committed to excellence and maintaining the public trust. To this end, we launched an agency-wide initiative aimed at addressing workplace culture issues, beginning with identifying our core values from the ground up. After conducting numerous employee surveys and nineteen focus groups touching every component of our workforce, we identified the following six fundamental core values that govern our deliberations, inform our decision-making, and guide our actions: accountability, diversity, equity, excellence, integrity, and transparency. These values served as the framework for our agency's strategic planning.

Within the FDA, the Office of Equal Employment Opportunity and Diversity Management (OEEODM) is the lead organizational entity responsible for promoting two of the key values: diversity and equity. As such, it was important that we develop our own EEO and Diversity Management Strategic Action Plan to operationalize these values in the agency. To do so, we had to begin with a vision.

Our Vision: The Business Case for Diversity

It is our vision in OEEODM that equal employment opportunity and diversity management are separate but symbiotic functions essential to the success of FDA as a high performing organization. One cannot thrive without the other, and equity in the workplace must be the foundation upon which institutional diversity can be built. We promote both the ethical as well as the business case for promoting equity and diversity in the FDA culture. To fully appreciate the business case for diversity, we must define diversity broadly beyond race and gender to include all that makes us unique, including our cognitive, intellectual, and philosophical perspectives.

The concept of diversity has gone through several iterations since its inception in the civil rights movement in the 1960s. It was followed by affirmative action in the 1970s and evolved into diversity management in the 1990s, largely through the writings of Dr. Roosevelt Thomas.[3] Today, industry is motivated by the business case for diversity, a concept we have championed in the FDA and beyond. The business case for diversity can be

---

[3] R. Roosevelt Thomas Jr., *Beyond Race and Gender: Unleashing the Power of Your Total Workforce by Managing Diversity* (New York: AMACOM, 1991).

made on several levels: the high cost of attrition due to disengaged employees; the competitive advantage in having diverse personnel connecting with diverse markets and increasing market share; and the performance advantages of leveraging the varied skills, talent, and perspectives of a diverse workforce. Our business case focuses on the last aspect: capitalizing on diversity to maximize performance.

What Does the Research Show?

Before we began to champion the business case for diversity, we wanted to know what the research had to say. While data should never be the exclusive driver of social change, it does play a compelling role in making the case. What we found was that research supports the thesis that diversity offers measurable advantages to an organization's performance and productivity. Empirical studies demonstrated that, under facilitating conditions, workforce diversity is positively correlated with higher performance outcomes and greater economic returns.

The Diversity Research Network conducted a five-year longitudinal study on the *Effects of Workforce Diversity on Business Performance*.[4] It performed in-depth studies of Fortune 500 companies and found that workforce diversity is positively associated with high performance outcome measures. Specifically, it found that racial diversity was positively associated with high-performance outcome measures in organizations that "integrate and leverage diverse perspectives" as resources for product delivery. It also found that gender diversity yielded more effective group processes and performance in organizations with "people-oriented" performance cultures. Interestingly, both of these results were highly dependent on the presence of "facilitating" or "inhibiting" conditions in the work culture; otherwise, the outcomes were reversed. In this regard, emerging research is demonstrating the link between perceptions of fairness in the workplace and employee engagement. Researchers are finding a quantifiable correlation between employees' perception of being treated fairly and their corresponding levels of engagement, morale, and conversely "burnout" in the workplace.[5]

---

[4]Diversity Research Network, *The Effects of Diversity on Business Performance* (Wiley Periodicals, November 2002).
[5]Christina Maslach and Michael Leiter, "Early Predictors of Job Burnout and Engagement," *Journal of Applied Psychology*, June 2008.

Similarly, the Center for Creative Leadership conducted a study on team dynamics and work productivity that showed that diverse teams were more creative and performed better than homogenous teams.[6] In the economic terms, a major study of diversity was conducted in 2001 that analyzed employer and employee data of more than 20,000 business establishments in the manufacturing, retail, and service commercial sectors.[7] In summary, the study revealed that racial and gender diversity was positively correlated with establishment productivity, product quality, and economic return on investment.

The research suggests that workforce diversity pays economic dividends, but requires investment, as well. Such investment must take the form of outreach, EEO compliance activities, training, employee development, diversity management programming, responsive employee benefits, work-life balance, mentoring/succession planning, conflict management programs, etc. Organizational leadership, EEO, and HR offices shoulder a major part of the responsibility in delivering on the promise that may be implied by this research. Leaders must "walk the talk" and HR and EEO practitioners must implement responsive and strategically aligned recruitment and retention strategies that comport with the mission of the organization.

I believe "diversity of thought" is the next natural evolution of the diversity management continuum. Through research, we have demonstrated that the competitive advantage of workforce diversity is not limited to differentiating products to appeal to emerging markets. It also results from leveraging an organization's collective intellectual capital to anticipate market needs. It is important that we recognize the unbreakable link of diversity of thought to our human identity. Our thoughts, beliefs, and perspectives are in great measure a product of our personal histories and sociological profile. When we make this link, we are able to marshal commitment (financial and otherwise) for diversity in its traditional context—a true win-win scenario for organizations. By marketing this

---

[6] *Work Team Dynamics and Productivity in the Context of Diversity Conference* (Center for Creative Leadership, N.Y.U., A.P.A., October 1994).
[7] Linda Barrington and Kenneth Trosky, *Workforce Diversity and Productivity: An Analysis of Employer-Employee Matched Data* (The Conference Board, April 2001).

vision of diversity, we have rendered it universally inclusive, and thus relevant to all segments of our society and workforce.

Our Mission: Protect and Empower Our Human Resources

Guided by a vision, we proceeded with articulating the mission of OEEODM. As a public service agency, we know we cannot tolerate barriers to equal employment opportunity that exclude large segments of society and disenfranchise members of our workforce. It is critical that we leverage diverse perspectives, enable constructive dissent, and manage conflict effectively and efficiently. To that end, OEEODM's mission is to protect individuals' rights to equal employment opportunity, promote diversity, and empower individuals so that they may contribute to their fullest potential in support of the FDA's mission.

In developing our EEO and Diversity Management Strategic Action Plan, it was important we consider of all of our stakeholders, especially our employees. The plan must be, in large measure, the product of those responsible for implementing it in order to engender ownership. To accomplish this, we organized our staff into cross-functional teams and spent weeks benchmarking the best practices in both the public and the private sectors. We then came together as a group at a multi-day retreat and facilitated our own strategic planning work session. We reviewed the research and proceeded to draft mission-oriented goals, corresponding objectives, and action-oriented strategies to implement them. Finally, we identified performance metrics that would gauge our performance on these objectives.

Our efforts culminated in a multi-year EEO and Diversity Management Strategic Action Plan that contains an array of cutting-edge strategies that resulted in FDA being recognized as a model EEO program and Leading Agency in Diversity Management Practices.[8] We later complemented our plan with an *Annual EEO & Diversity Management Performance Report* that reports on the efficacy of our planning efforts. Some of our initiatives and best practices include the following:

---

[8] *Diversity Management: Expert-Identified Leading Practices and Agency Examples* (U.S. GAO, January 2005).

Strategies and Best Practices

- Multi-year EEO and Diversity Strategic Action Plan
- *Annual EEO & Diversity Management Performance Report*
- Diversity-focused Recruitment Outreach and Retention Plan
- Strategic partnerships/memoranda of understanding with diverse institutions of higher education and professional associations to build pipelines to the agency
- Diversity-focused succession planning
- Diversity-focused leadership development and employee mentoring programs
- Diversity-focused internship/fellowship programs to build diverse scientific recruitment pipelines
- Guide to Conducting a Fair and EEO Compliant Selection Process for managers
- Conflict Prevention and Resolution Program aimed at early, constructive dispute resolution to address any workplace conflict
- Web-based EEO complaints management, alternative dispute resolution, and reasonable accommodation case tracking systems
- Internal complaints processing standard operating procedures
- Leadership briefings on the Business Case for Diversity
- Diversity climate survey and focus groups
- Agency-wide Diversity Council
- Annual Leadership Diversity Summit
- Creation of Shared Leadership, Diversity in Action, and Excellence in Equity awards
- Mandatory EEO and Diversity Training for managers and supervisors
- Mandatory online EEO/No FEAR Training for all Employees
- Cross-functional teams and universal/generalist position descriptions

What Gets Measured Gets Done

Measurement is an essential component in effective strategic planning. It is the engine that drives the plan. Metrics reveal the success (or failure) of our efforts. Every goal identified in the strategic plan must be accompanied by correlating objectives and implementing strategies. Strategies should be linked with appropriate metrics to determine whether you have reached your destination. To get the full picture, performance metrics must be a combination of output-based and outcome-based measures.

Output metrics measure the level of activity generated by the strategies: e.g., number of job fairs attended, number of training sessions conducted, number of employment applications processed, number of EEO complaints processed. Outputs can be valid indicators of levels of effort. They inform us about productivity for the purposes of resource allocation, business process improvement, and employee performance management.

We should look at output measures to make necessary adjustments to our processes and personnel. But they don't tell the whole story, or even the most important part of the story. The reason we engage in any mission is to achieve a desired end-state. Outputs do not measure end-states; outcomes do.

Output versus Outcome Measures

Outcome measures demonstrate the impact of our strategies on the achievement of our ultimate goals. In the HR/EEO context, they may include shortened hiring timeframes, increased representation of under-represented groups at all levels of the agency, increased levels of competencies in the agency, elimination of skills gaps, decline in complaints activity, higher retention rates, and higher employee engagement per survey results. All of these measure changes in the end-state and reflect the efficacy of our strategies in achieving our desired end-state.

Too often, public sector organizations focus exclusively on outputs and neglect outcome measures. As a result, we continue to pump limited resources year after year into ineffective programs and activities that, according to the relevant outcome data, are failing to achieve the goals of our mission. One illustration of this is the widening gap of low participation rates of Hispanics in the federal workforce, despite decades of affirmative recruitment efforts. For years, federal agencies have employed essentially the same recruitment outreach and retention strategies to increase Hispanic representation. Each year, we report these output metrics to the Office of Personnel Management (OPM) in the Federal Equal Opportunity Recruitment Program Report: the number of affinity group job fairs we attended, the number of job advertisements we posted, and the number of cultural observance programs we conducted. These measures inform OPM of our continuing and often repetitious efforts to close the gap in representation between our incumbent workforce and the available labor force.

However, if we look at the intended *outcome* measures, namely actual workforce representation, we see a more important story. As the graph below conveys, despite continuing investment in these traditional outreach and retention strategies, the data show we have *increased* instead of decreased the gap between Hispanic representation in the federal workforce and the civilian labor force over the last twelve years.

Hispanic Representation in the Workforce

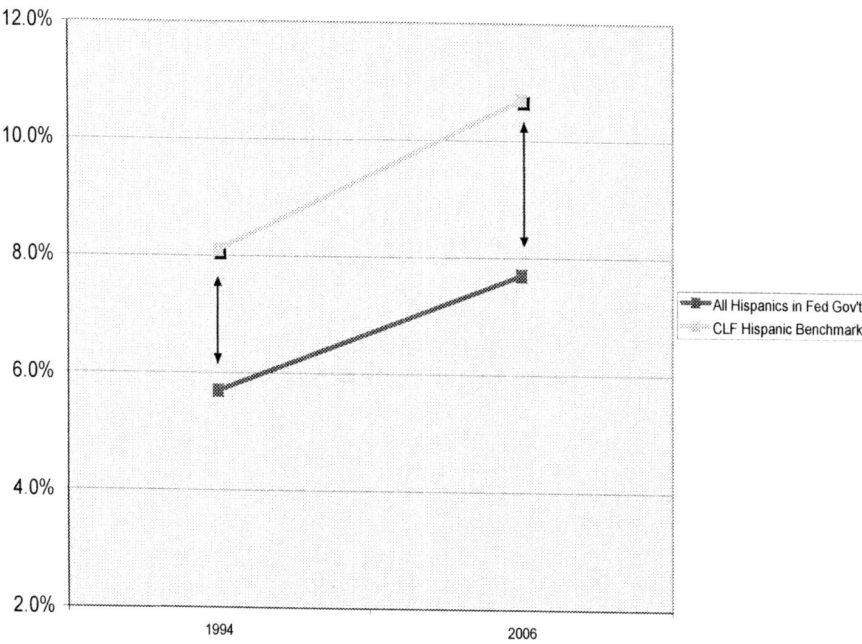

This is one illustration of the importance of planning, measurement, and reporting. While we have made considerable progress in other areas of workforce representation, this is one area where appropriate planning, measurement, and reporting could have informed our efforts and investments better. It also suggests we must think differently about our recruitment strategies. Perhaps attending the same generic job fairs where we find little return for our investment is not a prudent use of our limited resources. Perhaps we should instead focus on strategic partnerships with institutions of post-secondary education and professional associations focused on mission-critical occupations to build synergistic collaborations and mutually beneficial pipelines to our organizations.

At the FDA, we continue to pursue new partnerships with minority-serving institutions of higher education (Morehouse College, University of Puerto Rico) specializing in our scientific, mission-critical areas to generate internships, fellowships, faculty/staff exchanges, mentoring programs, and the like to build an ongoing collaboration and pipeline to our agency. Similarly, we developed new relationships with professional associations such as the National Medical Association representing African American physicians to promote diversity in our professional staff and advisory committees. We believe the metrics will show that these types of strategic collaborations will yield greater returns on our investment in workforce diversity.

Retention Strategies

Other retention strategies include a broad-based agency-wide diversity council with leadership, as well as employee, representation. We created this council as an advisory body reporting to the head of the agency on issues, concerns, and recommendations relating to workforce diversity in its broadest context. We also benchmarked and implemented internal standard operating procedures for EEO complaint processing based on best practices government-wide. This was coupled with the acquisition of state-of-the-art Web-based case management systems to efficiently track EEO complaints, alternative dispute resolution, and reasonable accommodations cases in compliance with all applicable laws and regulatory timeframes. We also developed first-time mandatory EEO compliance training for managers and supervisors to educate our supervisors on their legal and practical responsibilities in maintaining a discrimination- and harassment-free work environment. We complemented these strategies with a unique Conflict Prevention and Resolution Program that provides an array of proactive alternative dispute resolution strategies to resolve any workplace conflict.

As the graph below shows, these and other risk management/retention strategies have led to the dramatic decline in discrimination complaints over the past three years.

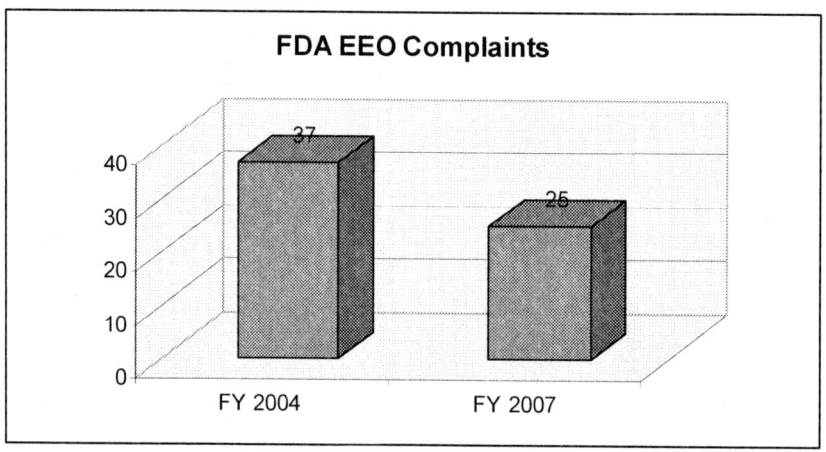

While we still have work to do, our measures in OEEODM suggest that we are on the right path. Within three years of planning, the metrics demonstrated the effectiveness of our planning. The FDA's formal discrimination complaint activity has steadily declined since we have implemented our strategies, and our workforce representation has marginally increased in most underrepresented areas. In addition, we are resolving higher rates of conflict in the workplace earlier, and at substantial cost savings to the agency.[9]

Unique Opportunities of the Future

Not since the Industrial Revolution has the American workplace had such a potent opportunity to reinvent itself. We have a unique opportunity to change our corporate paradigm, redesign our processes, and open the gates to infinite possibilities. We are on the cusp of a new era in organizational management, and HR and EEO have a pivotal role in ensuring we are equipped to meet the challenges that lie before us.

---

[9] *OEEODM Annual Performance Report for FY 2007* (FDA/OEEODM, January 2008).

Leaders bear a special obligation to promote a vision of excellence, fairness, and diversity in governance and industry. It is our responsibility to convey to our employees that they can be a part of something greater than themselves. They can be part of a great new enterprise that will transform the business of the world for a better quality of life for all.

When she wrote this chapter, Georgia Coffey was the director of the Office of Equal Employment Opportunity & Diversity Management for the U.S. Food and Drug Administration. She has more than twenty years of EEO, diversity, and civil rights experience in the public and private sectors.

During her tenure with the FDA, beginning in 2003, Ms. Coffey was recognized for creating the agency's first Diversity Council and Interagency Diversity Summit, implementing its first mandatory EEO compliance training for managers and supervisors, developing the agency's first EEO and diversity strategic action plan and annual performance report; developing an FDA diversity outreach and retention plan, developing guidance on conducting a fair and EEO-compliant selection process, and implementing numerous groundbreaking EEO and diversity initiatives for the FDA. In 2005, she served for six months as the acting assistant commissioner for management for the FDA.

Prior to joining the FDA, Ms. Coffey was the acting EEO and diversity manager for Montgomery County and served on the Montgomery County Commission on People with Disabilities, the Montgomery County Hate Violence Committee, the White House Initiative on Historically Black Colleges and Universities, and the Rockville Human Rights Commission, where she assisted in the creation of the city's first community mediation program.

Ms. Coffey has a bachelor's degree from the University of Maryland in psychology, a master's degree and doctoral work in education from American University, and a certificate in EEO studies from Cornell University's School of Industrial and Labor Relations. She is a native of Washington, D.C., and a wife and a mother of two children, and has devoted most of her adult work life to protecting the civil rights of individuals in the workplace.

Ms. Coffey recently became the deputy assistant secretary for diversity management and EEO at the U.S. Department of Veterans Affairs.

Aligning Your HR Plan with Business Goals and Core Performance Measures

Michael Cushing

Senior Vice President,

Resource and Information Management

Export-Import Bank of the United States

ASPATORE

Features of a Successful HR Strategy in Government Agencies

Although government is not a business, as a government corporation, we have a culture and mission similar to a private sector international financial institution. Essential to our success are recruiting, retaining, and developing talent and managing that talent for high performance.

A successful HR (human resources) strategy begins with answering the fundamental questions about our mission, business goals, and strategies. A good HR strategic plan depends on a good business strategic plan. Our business strategic plan should answer these questions:

- What's most important? What's our mission?
- What do we expect to achieve? Where do we want the business to be?
- How we will get there? We need a work plan and milestones.
- How we will measure how we're doing? At the top level, we focus on five measurement areas:
  - o Financial
  - o Productivity
  - o Customer satisfaction
  - o Cycle time
  - o Innovation and capability building

HR strategy starts with an HR strategic plan that is aligned with these corporate and business goals and performance measures. Once the strategic direction has been set, the next two tasks are to design the capabilities and manage service delivery. To that end, the HR strategic plan seeks to answer these questions:

- What kind of functions will we perform?
- What type of organization is the most effective for performing them?
- What kinds of skills are needed to perform those functions? We try to identify gaps in the skills we will need and the kinds of plans we can put into place to close those gaps.

Once an HR strategic plan has been adopted, we need to ensure that it can be successfully implemented, managed, and evaluated. Successful implementation requires elements of accountability, data measurement, and reporting. Working in partnership with the business line leaders, we want to make sure we have a measurement system in place in which we can measure the data that will tell us whether we are performing well. We also need a reporting mechanism that reports those performance data in a manner that is accessible and meaningful for the people who are accountable for the performance. Then we want to make sure that we provide feedback to everybody who is in some measure responsible for the HR plan. We communicate results to the process owners of both the business and the HR processes.

Changes and Developments over the Last Five Years

The first change is more integrated HR planning. Within agencies like ours, and probably also within the private sector, making sure that your HR plan is aligned with your entity's business strategies and core performance measures is very important. By that I mean you do not want an HR plan that is developed in isolation and that may even reflect best practices from the HR community, but that is not in sync with your business goals and performance measures. In the last five years, we have seen tighter integration and partnership between the HR functions and the business.

A second change is more attention to matching organizational design to business strategies. We have done a complete redesign of our organization, moving from a product line organization to what I call a business process structure, in which we are organized according to the various business processes we manage. In our case those business processes are transaction management, financial management, risk management, and operating or service management. A reorganization of this scope affects most of the professional staff, and we needed to do it without disrupting our business. We do about $12 billion worth of financial transactions a year, and we manage an asset portfolio of roughly $60 billion. We do that with about 450 people here in Washington and some field offices.

A third change is greater use of recruitment and retention incentives for our high-performing employees. This practice is standard in most comparable private sector institutions, but federal sector compensation policy has a long, and not distinguished, history of inflexibility. We have tried to base our employees' variable compensation more on their unique skills and value to the agency than on how long they have been here or what resources they might command—such as where they are within the management hierarchy. We try to look at what they bring to our company to meet our business goals. We do that in recruitment, to bring in new talent, and in retention, to hold onto key people.

Fourth, we focus more on our total compensation. Typically for our high-skill areas or top business line professionals—such as our loan officers, economists, and attorneys—our base pay and bonuses are less than these top performers could earn in the private sector financial services firms with which we compete. So to compete successfully, we need to offer broader compensation than base pay and bonuses. Hence, we offer a rewarding work life and a wide array of retirement and health benefits. Although we operate as a corporation, we offer government retirement and health benefits. As private sector retirement and health benefits have been both more uncertain and less rewarding, people have tended to look to us, especially mid-career employees. It's one of the few competitive advantages that the federal sector can offer.

Like many other corporations, we have also tried to offer the kind of workplace flexibility that will attract people who want to have interesting work, but are looking for more opportunities to have flexible work schedules. Traditionally flextime was code for women in the workplace, but we have found that interesting assignments, good training opportunities, and flexible schedules are incentives for younger-generation employees generally.

Finally, we have shifted from time-based and fixed pay to variable pay. We do work within a somewhat rigid and constrained governmental compensation structure, but within that structure we have tried to base pay more on how well employees have performed, and to make more of that pay variable and geared to individual performance that aligns with our overall corporate performance goals and metrics. Finally, we have put in place a new performance appraisal and performance measurement system for our most senior executives, which is aligned with our top-level corporate performance measures.

Measuring the Success of HR Strategies

We have four key indicators:

1. Employee satisfaction
2. Attrition in core professional series
3. Results in corporate performance measures
4. Compliance with laws and regulations

To measure employee satisfaction, we conduct annual employee satisfaction surveys that measure four areas:

1. Personal work experience
2. Recruitment, retention, and development
3. Performance management and incentives
4. Agency leadership

In analyzing the results of that survey, we look more at deviation and trends than absolute percentages because some numbers will always be relatively high and some relatively low. A high percentage of employees believe their work is important, enjoy their work, and feel they contribute. A smaller percentage of employees will tell you that the organization does a good job in managing poor performers. We look at where we deviate from other organizations of comparable size with comparable missions. Where are we much better than these organizations, and where are we much worse?

The result we analyze is trends over time. In what areas do we get better marks, and in what areas do our grades go down? Looking at our deviation and trends is a better indication of where we are doing well and where we need to focus.

The second key measure is attrition by career cohort in our core professional series. We have defined a number of professional series that have the skill sets that are most important to achieve success in the organization, and each quarter we measure what kind of attrition we have had in those series, both numbers and reasons.

We also try to measure by cohort—by types of people at various points in their careers. How are we doing at holding onto entry-level people? What's the attrition rate for mid-career people and for more senior people? In this respect lower is not necessarily a better number. Obviously high attrition in your core series, other than retirements, tells you that people are leaving your organization too fast, and you will have problems with knowledge transfer, institutional memory, and the right mix of skills. You also do not want zero attrition. If no one ever leaves the organization for any competing organization, it's an indication that we are over-paying or under-working.

Third, we look at the corporate performance measures I discussed earlier. The whole purpose of an HR strategy is to align with and support our corporate performance, so the extent that our corporate performance measures are doing well or not so well is an indication of how well our HR strategy is succeeding.

Finally, and one of the differences between managing in the government and private sectors, we measure our compliance with laws and regulations. Human resources policies and actions are subject to oversight by several congressional committees, an independent inspector general, several executive branch central management agencies that set government-wide standards, and two sets of independent external auditors. We review congressional and government-wide mandates and audit recommendations to assess our compliance.

Devising the best set of measures is a challenge, and always an exercise in balancing inherent tensions:

- *Alignment versus control.* Collectively the measures need to align with the strategy. Individually they need to be within control of the organization being measured.
- *Inclusiveness versus importance.* If you have too few, your measures won't map to your objectives. If you have too many, you won't have a meaningful dashboard for your managers.
- *Objective versus subjective.* Objective measures will miss important non-quantifiable goals. Subjective measures will be less fair and less manageable.

- *Currency versus stability.* If you revise measures infrequently, changes in priorities and external factors will make them less relevant. If you revise them too frequently, they will be seen as a burdensome exercise and lose support.

Trends That Will Affect HR

Two external demographic and economic trends will be important in the near future for our workforce planning and management. Conventional wisdom says that the most important trend will be a wave of retirements as baby boomers become eligible to retire. The prediction is for a massive loss of experienced talent and institutional knowledge and the need to recruit replacements. I'm in the minority in not expecting a retirement tsunami. Although we have many retirement-eligible employees, because of personal financial uncertainty and discouraging trends in the economy, many retirement-eligible employees are staying on, so the wave of retirements should very manageable.

Specifically in the financial services sector, the private sector's problems are our opportunity. As the financial industry downsizes and restructures, and private sector career paths become less certain, we have found it easier to recruit mid-career talent from financial service industries to come in to replace our departing employees, for reasons I mentioned having to do with our total compensation package. Trends in the economy at large and the financial industry will actually make it easier for us to get and keep talent, as opposed to some of the doomsayers who believe we will lose all of our talent and be unable to recruit replacements.

Michael Cushing is the senior vice president for resource and information management at the Export-Import Bank of the United States, a self-sustaining government corporation that finances the export of U.S. goods and services in international markets. The bank finances and insures more than $12 billion annually, does business in 120 countries, and manages an asset portfolio of $60 billion.

Mr. Cushing provides leadership for the organization's programs in human capital and strategic planning, information technology, and corporate operations. He has also served as the principal management official of three federal agencies. His private sector experience includes experience in asset management and investment development.

Mr. Cushing received a bachelor's degree from Harvard College and a law degree from Harvard Law School. The views expressed are his own.

Focusing on Internal Talent Development

Frank Guglielmo

Senior Vice President,
Leadership and Organizational Development
Interpublic Group

ASPATORE

My Role

I am the senior vice president responsible for the overall leadership development strategy of Interpublic Group. My team is responsible for directly providing tools and programs for executive development, supporting the chairman's office on a number of talent development initiatives, delivering expertise into our organization to improve organizational effectiveness, and running processes such as succession management.

The Context of Our Strategy

Interpublic Group is a Fortune 500 company and one of the world's largest marketing services and marketing communications companies. In 2007 we had approximately 42,000 employees and $6.5 billion in revenue. Communications and marketing services is essentially a professional services business. Our challenges are similar to those of companies in other professional services businesses; that is, we are a very talent-intensive business.

Successful HR strategies, particularly in professional services, typically have four core components: a focus on building an attractive employment value proposition that enables successful recruiting, a sophisticated approach to compensation, successful retention strategies, and a focus on internal talent development, which builds a deep pipeline of talent.

Waves of consolidations across the industry and the robust economy of the 1990s and early 2000s have lead many companies in the industry to focus much more heavily on recruiting and compensation strategies, often at the expense of retention and development efforts.

This trend is beginning to slow, and it is becoming easier to see a renewed focus on internal talent development. Shrinking labor pools, particularly in emerging markets such as India and China, as well as rapid technology change that is remaking the marketing services industry, have all placed a premium on the ability to grow and develop talent internally.

Our Successful Strategies

We have begun to develop a prospective on successful talent development strategies in professional services business, as illustrated in the chart below.

Characteristics of a "Professional Services" Organization	Implications for development in a "professional services" company	Talent Management Strategy Responses
↑ Moderately stable macro structure – tremendous fluidity of structure inside agencies	↑ Variability within standards – Client relationships and role differences within divisions require flexibility within standards	↑ Standards can be consistent in content but need to vary in execution to meet different agency cultures; role requirements will vary based client needs
↑ Primary value lies in the individual talent	↑ Remaining expert in one's profession is critical; limited focus on management/leadership capabilities until senior roles are reached	↑ Management/leadership development will require an enterprise level focus as local offices will naturally defer this in favor of professional development
↑ Processes and Products provide incremental value, amplifying value of individuals	↑ Roles cannot be used as primary source of development – i.e., clients will not tolerate an individual having a learning curve in a role and not performing at 100% on day one	↑ Individuals will need to be ready for new positions before they are promoted – on the job learning will need to be focused on deepening experience rather than building skills
↑ Projects are of variable length and are extended, enlarged, contracted or shortened continuously	↑ Career time horizons are short to moderate	↑ Continuous career conversations and planning for next career moves need to take precedence over career ladders and long-term career planning
↑ Unplanned business disruptions are constant (e.g., client wins and losses, game changing technologies, new competitors)	↑ Continuous learning is required as adaptability to changing conditions is key	↑ Learning needs to become a cultural imperative
↑ An employee's value is a function of their individual talent rather than knowledge of or time with the agency, allowing individuals easy mobility across agencies	↑ Easy mobility of talent leads to foreseeable, predictable attrition	↑ Foreseeable attrition requires having a plan for a pipeline of new talent as well as quality decision making to ensure consistently high quality of talent

This perspective paints a picture of a highly fluid, rapidly changing organizational environment, which would be familiar to anyone who has worked in a professional services organization. It suggests that the best human resources strategic response to this environment is to focus on building flexibility and adaptability into the workforce. Our efforts to create this type of flexibility have centered on three things: building programs and strategies guided by principles rather than rules, having the resources in place to deeply prepare individuals for new responsibilities, and having the tools to identify and reward talented individuals, maintaining a continuous pipeline of talent throughout the organization.

Two strategic initiatives we have undertaken over the last several years illustrate the application of these ideas. One was a revamping of our executive compensation programs, which has been extremely successful. This change involved a decided shift away from profit sharing and toward incentive-based compensation. Our executives now have incentive targets, and actual rewards vary, based on individual and organizational performance in a wide range of areas including profitability, strategic objectives, diversity, and talent management.

Rather than having "retroactive" compensation, i.e., distributing bonuses based on year-end profit levels, we are taking a proactive stance. We help guide behavior and continually fine-tune the direction of the organization by telling leaders that they can earn incentives based on their success in delivering certain objectives that drive the companies' long- and short-term success. This is not a particularly new concept, but it has been remarkably successful in helping shape the success of the company.

The second strategic initiative that we have driven over the last three to four years is the introduction of a version of a succession management processes across the globe. In our organization, we call it Talent Review. Talent Review has focused on identifying critical individuals, placing a focus on their development, and putting them in increasing positions of responsibility. We can get a sense of the organization and understand where our capability gaps are, so we can form proactive plans to address them.

Our Talent Review process has yielded a number of real benefits. We have been able to extend substantially the "talent fluency"—the breadth of knowledge regarding the talented individuals in the organization—of our executives. We have been able to connect talented, high-potential leaders across the organization to executive management and the board. Finally, by connecting action plans identified during the annual Talent Review process to the executive incentive compensation program, we have been able to place talent development and building a pipeline of talent front and center in the company.

The Role of Employees

To be successful, our actions have to be line-driven. Our Talent Review process is purely a line-led effort. It involves absolute ground-up work from local market leaders, regional leaders, and operating division CEOs.

We have a very active chairman and board of directors. They all take a direct hand in our talent development efforts. For example, our chairman took almost thirty-five hours of meetings with various operating company heads focused on our succession management and Talent Review process this year.

Measuring Success

Our most important measure is the success of the company. We have seen gratifying increases in both our margin and revenue performance over the last several years. We have been able to build a culture where we have significantly moved toward internal promotion, rather than external hiring, in our senior and executive ranks across the organization. This change has led to greater stability and an even larger focus on longer-term strategic initiatives.

Best Practices

Interpublic Group is a holding company that owns a large number of marketing communication companies, each with unique brand identities and go-to-market strategies. As a total enterprise, our operating values are transparency, internal collaboration, and flexible architecture. These values imply that we deal openly with our clients and with each other and that our organizational structure shouldn't get in the way of delivering services or meeting client needs. We are trying to bridge different operating divisions, some of whom are competitors, to create the best solutions for our clients and the most creative, successful environments for our employees.

My department sits at the Interpublic Group, holding-company level. Our essential operating philosophy is "large company developed small company solutions." We take the resources and the capabilities that a Fortune 500 company can muster and use them to build solutions that are appropriate for our agencies and advertising networks, which range in size from extremely large businesses to small businesses. We build and distribute tools and resources to a large number of advertising agencies and marketing companies in ways that they can digest. We want to find ways to leverage our capability to deliver solutions that each of our agencies can use independently, but few of them could build independently.

Essential Research

It is critically important for us to meet client expectations. We are a purely client-driven business. Our major product is creativity. Creativity is what we sell and deliver for our clients. With any new HR initiative or strategy, our first question is: How it is going to help local agencies for our global networks best deliver for our clients.

Our essential research involves talking to agency executives and line leaders—the people who are directly involved with developing solutions for clients. We also speak with clients to gain their perspectives on the types of capabilities we as a company need to develop.

The Role of the Internet

We recently launched what I consider a highly sophisticated HR endeavor to address the issue of improving leadership capabilities. As a professional services company, the vast majority of our staff are billable and directly accountable for clients. Taking them out of their roles and into a classroom or another traditional development event is difficult because they need to be responsive to the clients. They have high-pressure jobs with long hours. As a global company, with the majority of our workforce outside the United States, we needed to be able to transcend the limitations of being dispersed. At the same time, as a highly creative group of people, we know the power, energy, and learning that occur through interpersonal interactions. And we know that experience is the most effective way of learning.

Some of these forces argue for a distance-learning approach to leadership training, while others argue for an in-person, highly interactive learning environment. We solved this problem by creating a new type of global leadership development program we call "MyLead."

In conjunction with a partner, Fenestra, we have built an interactive development experience that involves an online-delivered assessment center style simulation. This includes everything from interactive e-mail and voicemail to documents and contact lists delivered to the participant on a faux computer "desktop" to a live phone bank team who interact as role players. Our role players are highly trained and are supported by a CRM (customer relationship management) system that allows them to continue an ongoing dialogue with a participant over a series of phone calls and e-mails over a number of weeks to address issues in the simulation. Role players and individual coaches provide ongoing detailed feedback to participants about their leadership capabilities. The coaches spend five one-hour coaching sessions with each participant, who also has access to online learning content, development planning, and self assessment tools, all delivered through the same online platform.

The program lasts for seven weeks and allows individuals to work at their own pace. The simulation challenges are adjustable to each individual's development plan and skill level. We have had tremendous success with the program all over the world. It has been hugely successful in China, India, and some of our other Asian markets where travel to training programs is impractical. We have had MyLead in place for a year, and close to 300 people have participated. I have been doing this for twenty-five years, and it is one of the most innovative solutions I have ever seen.

Future Strategies

Building on the work that we have done, the next big place we need to move into is becoming increasingly sophisticated around issues of career development. Our industry in general and our company in particular skew to a younger demographic. We have many Generation Y people all over the world. There is a strong interest and willingness on their part to manage their own careers and to be engaged in the process.

Our next challenge is to find a way for the company to be more meaningfully engaged with employees in their career decisions and explorations. Our efforts will be three-pronged. First, we have to find ways to arm leaders to thoughtfully engage the people around them in career conversations. Next, we have to arm individuals with the skills and knowledge to think about their careers in ways that are longer-term. Third, we have to implement organizational policies and systems that allow the most practically open talent market inside the organization.

It is not always practical for an organization to have a fully open labor market internally, especially at a holding company where divisions compete with each other in the marketplace. There are limitations, but within the boundaries of practicality, we will be looking for ways to open our internal labor market. The extent to which we can reduce turnover and have individuals begin to consider the family of Interpublic companies as their primary hunting ground for new opportunities will be our measure of success.

Budgeting

My department's entire budget is allocated to implementing HR strategies. Everyone in HR at the holding-company level in Interpublic Group is 100 percent focused on global HR strategies. At the local division level, there is a mix of daily execution of HR tasks, which consume 70 percent of activities, and 30 percent broader strategic activities.

Upcoming Trends

The biggest industry trend for us is the continued digitalization of media. More and more media are becoming Web-delivered. A tremendous growth of devices allows wireless or broadband communications from anywhere. People have greater control of the messages they receive. As clients look to us to provide creative, innovative ways to develop and communicate messages to consumers in this rapidly changing environment, we have a greater need than ever to create a culture of continuous learning and development.

Frank Guglielmo is senior vice president, leadership and organizational development, at the Interpublic Group of Companies, where he has been since 2004. In this role he is responsible for the companies' overall leadership development and talent management strategies.

Mr. Guglielmo has twenty years of experience in leading efforts to build individual and organizational capabilities. Prior to joining Interpublic, he was managing director at Park Consulting, focusing on leadership development, assessment, and succession management. He has also been director, management and organizational development, at Altria Corporate Services Inc. and vice president, branch management selection and development, at Prudential Securities. In both of these roles, Mr. Guglielmo was accountable for leading efforts in management selection and development, high-potential development, and succession management. He began his career as a senior consultant at Applied Research Corporation, a consulting firm specializing in management assessment and development.

Mr. Guglielmo holds both an M.S. and a Ph.D. in organizational psychology. He has conducted training programs and organizational interventions in many countries in Europe and Latin America, as well as the United States. He is a member of the American Psychological Association and the Metropolitan New York Association for Applied Psychology.

Driving Business Outcomes through Cultural Alignment

Thomas A. Fentner

Senior Vice President,
Human Resources and Administrative Services
HealthNow New York Inc.

ASPATORE

Defining Success

Successful companies begin with a clear, concise mission statement complemented by a vision for the future. Equally important is the development of corporate values—loosely defined as "the way we do things around here." A strategic plan is then developed, which includes a realistic view of the competitive environment and strengths, weaknesses, opportunities, and threats the company will face over the next three to five years. Goals and strategies are then developed to guide the execution and measure progress. Since the actual implementation of any strategic or operating plan depends on the people charged with executing the plan, it is critically important that a well-developed HR (human resources) strategy be aligned with the strategic plan.

A well-developed HR strategy must be in complete alignment with the mission, vision, and values so that a macroscopic organizational view could trace a line of sight directly from the mission, vision, and values of a business straight through every piece of the operation that affects the workforce. Too often, companies develop values that sound good but have little or no meaning, since the corporate actions are not in alignment with the value statements. When misalignment occurs at a strategic level, the problems trickle down to levels of operations and implementation, where pieces of strategy disconnect.

Misalignment is always a concern for HR departments; though the most important ingredient in mixing a successful HR strategy is this fundamental agreement in direction and philosophy, one encounters HR misalignment in companies far more often than perfect alignment. Without a unified strategy, there can be no unified practice, and practices out of alignment with company values reduce those values to mere words on paper, thus creating confusion and morale issues at the staff level.

Strategic Success and HealthNow

HealthNow, with corporate headquarters located in Buffalo, New York, is the parent company of BlueCross BlueShield of Western New York, Blue Shield of Northeastern New York, and Brokerage Concepts Inc. HealthNow annual revenues exceed $2 billion, with an employee population of 2,500. Since 1936, HealthNow has been an innovator in providing quality health care services to companies and individuals.

I was recruited to HealthNow in the summer of 2006 to assist with the design, development, and implementation of a new business model. The new business model included the following components:

- Organizational redesign to place the right people in the right places at the right times necessary to deliver legendary service to our customers
- Redesign of policies, procedures, and metrics to meet the needs of our customers
- Alignment of talent to meet and exceed customer expectations
- Enhancement of communications, internal and external, including methods, customization, content, and clarity

My responsibilities as SVP of human resources include all programs and services that serve to "Find, Launch, Develop, Differentiate, and Retain the organizational talent necessary to drive our competitive advantage."

The foundation of our new business model is "to revolutionize the organizational culture such that it becomes HealthNow's competitive advantage." It was clear to us that any industry competitor can duplicate products, services, pricing, etc., but a corporate culture dedicated to delivering legendary service could not be duplicated and would become a competitive advantage.

Once it was clear where we needed to be, we made an assessment of where we were and identified the gap that needed to be addressed. Often, when pressed, one finds that businesses are out of alignment in that the actual culture operates much differently from the words contained in the mission, vision, and especially values as proclaimed by the organization. It is extraordinarily important to conduct an in-depth assessment of every policy, procedure, employee event, etc. to determine alignment, and, most importantly, those areas out of alignment need to be addressed quickly with key message points.

As we embarked on the creation of a new business model, we made a conscientious effort to clearly define the values that would completely support the new business model and bring it to life:

HealthNow New York Inc. *Core Values: "How we do what we do"*

- *RESPECT*
  Treat everyone with courtesy and dignity
- *PERSONAL RESPONSIBILITY*
  Accountability for delivering results
- *EXCELLENCE*
  Pursuit of exceptional performance
- *TEAMWORK*
  Together we succeed
- *PASSION*
  Enthusiasm makes the difference
- *INTEGRITY*
  Behaving honestly, fairly, and ethically

Even an aggressive culture change cannot be considered complete in less than three years, and typically five years will elapse before most such organizational shifts can be evaluated for success. At HealthNow, our new business model required us to shift the culture from that of an organization focused internally to an organization focused on meeting and exceeding the needs of the customer. The ultimate measure of the success is our ability to attract new customers while retaining and growing the existing customer base and improving customer satisfaction levels.

Best Practices in HR Strategy

Human resources departments frequently fall into the trap of monopolizing staff capacity with administrative duties. At HealthNow, our focus is on creating self-service administrative modules that free HR professionals to assist, advise, and generally leverage themselves within the company, yielding more value. We have a professional staff member of HR on the leadership team dedicated to each of our strategic business units and corporate functions. Our HR professionals actively participate in business decisions and strategy discussions, helping line executives achieve their goals.

The business model within HR aligns with the business model of the company in that the customer is the center of all we do. In the case of HR, we have "internal customers," who are the management and staff we serve, and we have "outside customers," represented by applicants, vendors, consultants, contractors, and so on. Our major touch point between the customer and HR is the HRC (human resources consultant), as depicted in our Customer Service Model, illustrated on the next page. Although members of the HR staff, these individuals are expected to be totally aligned with and members of the business units they serve. They in turn are customers of the corporate HR staff, who exist to support their needs.

This service model allows each business to have a single touch point between the services provided by HR and the business. The HRC is expected to be the liaison between the business and HR and work with corporate HR to deliver the programs and services necessary to meet and exceed the needs of the business.

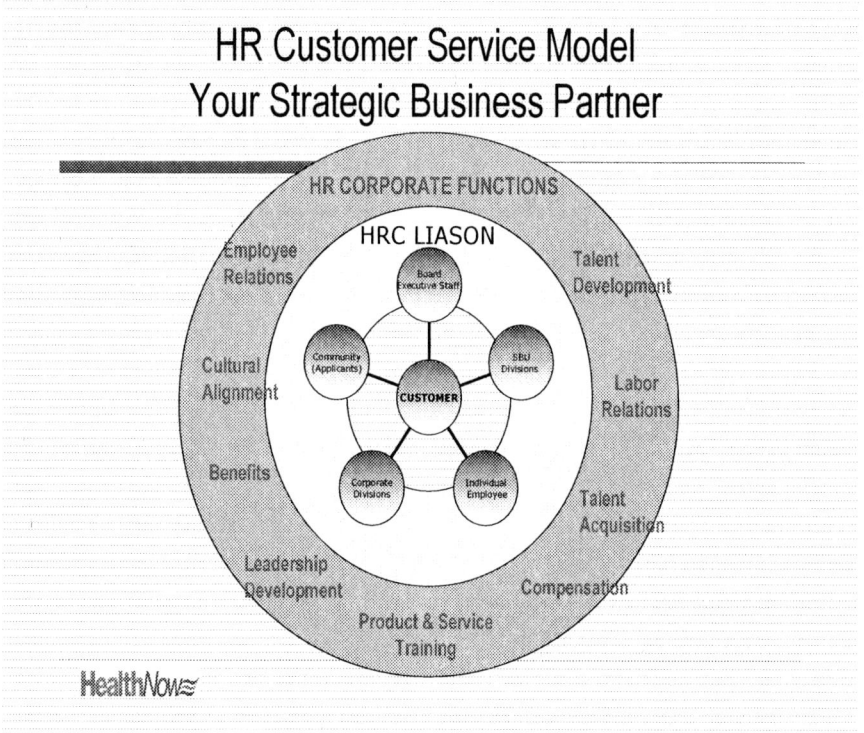

One area where we spend considerable time and effort to support a culture change is in the talent acquisition process. It is critical that we seek the talent who have both the subject matter and the technical expertise necessary to do the job, but it is equally or more important to hire individuals aligned with our values. HealthNow's practices differ from some other companies' hiring methods through our audacious and exacting talent acquisition process. We set high standards, and we do expect potential team members to meet and exceed those standards. Although it is reasonably easy to assess technical skills and experience, it is much more difficult to assess things like alignment with core values and overall attitude.

At HealthNow we employ a rigorous testing procedure to determine alignment with our corporate values and the overall attitude of a prospective candidate. HealthNow's hiring practices are considerably more selective than those used in companies that seek to simply fill a position, to hire for a certain technical expertise, for X years of experience accompanied by Y degree. At HealthNow our focus is an equal combination of technical skill, attitude, and alignment with core values. We believe with these attributes, we can develop new hires from the inside into subject matter experts. Talent and the alignment of that talent with corporate mission, vision, and values are critical issues for overall business success.

Employee Accountability

At HealthNow, every employee is responsible and accountable for meeting the standards as outlined in our core values. In developing the values, management created the framework and solicited the input from the entire employee base to describe the behaviors they believed would best exhibit the meaning of the value. The collective input was refined and incorporated in the final description. Employees recognized their input and endorsed the final value description. The performance review process includes a section dedicated to performance against regular job duties, as well as a section dedicated to performance against the behaviors associated with the core values. This performance is reviewed regularly and is considered for determining promotions, as well as other development opportunities. It is critical that all decisions, policies, and procedures are in perfect alignment with the values for the values to drive a consistent culture.

Likewise, our executive leadership team, through our front-line supervisors, is accountable for "walking the talk" with respect to the core values. This alignment is critical as employees observe the behaviors of the leadership team and assess whether they practice what they preach.

A real test for an organization is how to deal with an extremely talented individual who has unique skills or experience and does not comply with the core values—will the organization hold that person to the same standards or look the other way? The employee staff, as well as the rest of the management team, looks for these situations to assess whether the organization really believes in its values, or they are simply words on paper to be observed by some while others are not accountable. The organization must recognize that a culture will form from either situation. At HealthNow, no person is larger than our culture, regardless of skill set or experience. We believe our values form the platform for the way we do business, and that will not be compromised. Our decisions, policies, and procedures consistently and constantly stream the message that our values form the basis for everything we do.

Alignment with core values at HealthNow flows from the top of the hierarchy down to the individual employee level, ensuring that leaders are well-versed in appropriate business direction, as well as behaviors. We expect this alignment to result in consistency in meeting and exceeding the needs of our customers.

On Research and an HR Strategy

I find a strong network of HR executives to be the best source for researching best practices in HR strategy. I always prefer to talk to an executive who is living it, as opposed to a consultant who is preaching it. Best practices are usually the safest and most effective resource for implementing new HR strategies. Attending high-level conferences allows me to meet with other practitioners in the industry, learn which practices they employ, gain exposure to different ideas, and profit from the experiences of others regarding the efficacy of their techniques. A practitioner must deal with the real-life variables that don't exist in the pure environment of a consultant; the practitioner, therefore, has a more realistic view of the challenges associated with designing and implementing HR strategy.

Best practice benchmarking is a resource of increasing value, as HR has become steadily more quantified and measurable in the past decade, and as

Internet research yields data fresher and easier to acquire than ever. It is important to be selective with the metrics you choose to benchmark against. I prefer a dashboard approach of a limited number of metrics that truly measure our progress.

Networking groups are another resource of note for HR best practices clues. In Western New York, top HR executives from the top twenty companies meet quarterly, representing a number of different industries, and discuss major HR issues common to all. Cutting-edge thinking can be found in such gatherings, and exposure to issues from different sectors—such as international business, for example—can often provide useful perspectives for strategizing internally. This network provides a real resource and an opportunity to collaborate on various issues that affect the community as a whole and our profession.

A Perfect Fit: HR Business Partner

Strategic alignment, ensured by HR practices, influences business success overall, even at the level of product or service development. It is incumbent upon HR professionals to understand the business—what drives the market, where revenue comes from, what market share is, who the competitors are, how margin is generated, etc. To create the value proposition for the business, the HR professional must understand how the business works and how his or her work in HR contributes to the success of the business.

The major product line of HealthNow is health insurance. Although we service individual customers, a significant part of our insurance business is purchased by companies on behalf of their respective employee populations. In most cases, especially for larger companies, the purchasing customer is the leadership of the HR function within that company. As an HR executive, I have been in the situation of purchasing insurance for employees of large companies and now use that knowledge to help HealthNow address the issues important to HR executives. In some cases, this involves engaging in sales calls and discussions with the company HR executives and assisting them in providing quality coverage for their employee populations at cost-effective prices. We are able to bring a team of professionals, including HR input, to the customer and create a value proposition to meet and exceed the needs of the customer.

Whatever the business, the HR professional needs to understand the business drivers so they can position HR strategy to complement and influence business outcomes. The credibility of the HR function is predicated on understanding the business and more importantly, how the understanding translates into actions that have a positive impact on business outcomes.

Budgeting for HR Strategy

The HR budget can be split between administrative costs and strategic initiatives. On the administrative side we consider the salaries and programs essential to the day-to-day operation of the department. Our focus is employee self-service, and our challenge is to continue to find ways of delivering routine information to employees on a self-service basis. This enables the employees to get the information when they need it and is much more cost-effective for the organization. At this point, approximately 60 percent of HealthNow's HR budget is dedicated to the administrative costs of operating the HR function.

The strategic side includes various testing and assessment tools, surveys, research and development—leadership as well as individual. We have a major focus on acquiring the right talent, and more importantly, once we have that talent, how we retain it. HR strategy, research, and evaluation make up roughly 20 percent of our budget, which may not be wholly reflected in money spent, since much of our research involves networking and attending conferences to learn best practices. The remaining 20 percent is focused on development, which includes an extensive online university, leadership development programs, conferences, seminars, and an on-site library in each of our five major locations that allows members of the management team a physical place to focus on research and analysis without constant interruption.

It is a healthy exercise for every HR executive to look at the operating budget and consider how to reduce the administrative costs within HR so that, on a percentage basis, more of the HR annual operating budget is spent on strategic HR issues as opposed to administrative HR issues.

A Look to the Future: The Coming Year for HR at HealthNow

HealthNow is evolving; although we are still in the business of providing health insurance, we are increasingly focused on becoming more of a strategic partner for our customers and the community we serve, while creating a value proposition based on improving the health, and therefore quality of life, for our customers.

As we edge further into these responsibilities, our talent acquisition and development strategies must reflect the changes in company role and direction, producing hybrid consultant/partnership experts who can help customers drive their own health experiences. As claim information becomes more sophisticated and readily available and useful, customers will benefit increasingly from a clinical perspective and counsel on conditions precipitating frequent claims and, more importantly, the interventions that can positively affect behavior, rather than the traditional insurance sales-driven model, which offered only cost and implementation advice. Our focus in the coming year will be geared toward training our internal clinicians on how to partner with the customer and use data to influence positive changes in behavior.

In addition, we will focus on the professional development of internal staff both from a leadership perspective and from an individual contributor perspective. Recognizing that talent drives business outcomes, we need to focus on a more sophisticated model of identifying internal talent and establishing a formalized approach to their development. This is accomplished by specific job rotations, outside development programs, internal project assignments, and opportunities at all levels in the organization.

A third major initiative will be to explore non-traditional work arrangements, including telecommuting, working at home, non-traditional hours/days, and various configurations. We need to put some flexible framework around these work arrangements with the focus on creating an environment that will allow us to tap into the talent (both current and new) who are unable or unwilling to work the traditional work week.

Evaluating Future Success

The measure for success is best demonstrated by the direct impact on the business. If we believe our competitive advantage comes from our staff, then the approach to building a culture that will retain and attract top talent will be measured by the success of the business, as measured by market share, growth in new business with retention of existing business, growth in margin, and growth in reserves. Unless results are measured through the business outcome, there is no alignment between the role of HR and the value added to the company.

HR Strategy: A Projection

Our new HR strategies should provide HealthNow with a competitive advantage in our market in the future. The health insurance industry is changing. Health insurance was near the top of the list of domestic agenda items in the 2008 presidential election. The number of uninsured people, the cost of health care, and other related problems are driving questions for all businesses, and we need to be the answer for our customers; we need to partner with them, and our strategies need to propel us toward that end. More and more companies will be looking for health insurance answers in the future, and HealthNow's superior talent and creative, customer-centered problem-solving will lower costs, attract and retain customers, and be our competitive advantage.

Thomas A. Fentner is senior vice president, human resources and administrative services, for HealthNow New York Inc. He has held this position since 2006.

Prior to joining HealthNow, Mr. Fentner served as an HR consultant from 2004 to 2006. During this time, he consulted for The Hunter Group (Navigant Consulting) on hospital turn-around projects in Indiana, Illinois, Connecticut, and New York. He served as interim chief HR officer for Westchester Medical Center in a turnaround that took the hospital from a loss of $100 million in 2003 to breaking even in 2006. He also negotiated more than ten labor agreements for various clients.

Prior to this, he was selected senior vice president, human resources, for the newly formed Kaleida Health System. The system consists of Buffalo General, Millard Fillmore Gates, Millard Fillmore Suburban, Women's and Children's Hospital, and DeGraff Memorial Hospital. Reporting to System's CEO, Mr. Fentner designed, developed, and implemented a complete HR program for more than 13,000 employees. He served as chief negotiator for a master labor agreement that brought eighteen collective bargaining units, within five different unions, under a single agreement.

Mr. Fentner previously served as senior vice president, human resources, at Women and Children's Hospital of Buffalo. He began his career in 1971 at Goldome, where he reached the position of senior vice president, human resources, from 1987 to 1990.

Mr. Fentner attended the Graduate School of Finance and Management, Fairfield University, and received a Bachelor of Science degree in business from the Rochester Institute of Technology.

Ensuring Employee Buy-In before Implementing New HR Policies

Deborah J. Campbell

Deputy Superintendent

New York State Police

ASPATORE

Forming Our HR Department

Former Superintendent James McMahon established an Office of Human Resources for the New York State Police in 1994 and asked me to oversee its development. Prior to that, though we had programs for recruitment and Affirmative Action, we didn't have a formalized human resources department. The concept of human resources was foreign to most police agencies at that time. I believe that the field of policing was among the last sectors to recognize HR as an integral part of the organization.

At the time, several members of our agency had filed discrimination lawsuits, and Superintendent McMahon believed that it was important that our employees felt that we had appropriate mechanisms in place within the agency to deal with any issues or concerns that may arise. He discussed with me his idea of creating an Office of Human Resources and asked if I would be willing to accept the assignment as the first director. I received a very broad mandate in the beginning—all he stipulated was that human resources handle issues relative to recruitment, Equal Employment Opportunity, and career development to allow us to more effectively serve and develop our people.

As a full-service police agency, we are organized differently from many other agencies. We have approximately 5,000 sworn and 1,500 non-sworn (i.e., civilian) employees across the state of New York. Though our division headquarters is located in Albany, we occupy approximately 300 stations and provide police service to communities throughout the entire state of New York. Our organization is divided into ten troops, or central areas, statewide that report directly to division headquarters.

During the early stages of the development of our HR office, I felt the implementation of a new strategy such as this needed buy-in from the employees who would be directly affected by it. We began this process by selecting people to serve as part of a focus group, trying to be as inclusive as possible, ensuring the group consisted of both sworn and non-sworn employees of different ranks from the various troops and details statewide. This retreat was facilitated by IBM, with whom we had a strong working relationship. We brought all participants together at a remote location for a week to focus on our three primary missions: recruitment, EEO issues, and career development.

Addressing EEO Issues

We looked to our employees to tell us what they thought of the current mechanism in place to deal with issues involving possible discrimination or harassment, and whether they believed this was a problem within the agency. We learned that occasionally people did, in fact, feel that they were possibly discriminated against because of protected status, such as race or gender, but they were reluctant to report it because they didn't feel that the avenue in place was sufficient. At the time, employees would have to report violations to personnel at division headquarters through the Affirmative Action Office, or Internal Affairs. The only mechanism for handling such a complaint was through a formal investigation, which many people shied away from, as they did not want the stigma of being labeled a "complainer." Realizing the need to change the system, we next looked to best practices in other agencies.

We learned of a program utilized by the FBI that included both an informal resolution component (which would allow for mediation of issues), and a formal resolution component to the EEO process. This approach also used trained employees throughout the agency to work as EEO counselors, in an attempt to provide an alternative that employees would feel comfortable using.

After a site visit to FBI headquarters in Quantico, Virginia, where we learned more details of how the program worked, we realized that this process incorporated many of the things that our people had requested—an informal mechanism to deal with minor issues *before* they became more serious complaints and the use of trusted "peers" who would serve as mediators to facilitate this process. We tailored a program based on that model and developed a new policy for dealing with EEO issues whereby human resource counselors were the first point of contact in the case of an incident. We selected people within each troop and detail who were well-respected, and we provided them with comprehensive training, including an understanding of the EEO laws, diversity issues, and mediation skills.

Driving Buy-In

Most state police agencies are paramilitary in nature and deeply steeped in tradition. There is generally a pervasive attitude that, "This is the way we've done it. This is the way it has always been. This is the way that is best." Police agencies in particular can be slow to change and slow to embrace new ideas. I knew that as we formed human resources, one of the biggest obstacles would be getting the buy-in that we needed from our people.

I was fortunate in having the superintendent's support, as support from the top is essential with any major initiative like this one. If a new idea does not have the support from its top command staff, it has little chance of being successfully implemented. However, in addition to our executive staff located at division headquarters, each troop is led by a troop commander, who essentially commands approximately 400 sworn and non-sworn members. One of the things we tried to do early was to include the troop commanders in the new process and make sure that they understood it completely. We made it clear that we expected them to support the initiative. The confidential nature of the process was a big change for them, as they are accustomed to knowing everything that goes on within their troops, but we felt it was critical for success of the program. I was pleased with the support we received from this group, as the majority bought into the process immediately, which sent the message to the field personnel that this was a positive and necessary change.

It took almost a year to completely revamp this program and complete the necessary training, but I'm happy to say that the strategy has been very successful for us. We still occasionally have an employee file a lawsuit or action against the agency, but the majority of our employees choose to utilize our EEO process, many electing to have issues resolved informally. This allows the agency to identify small issues and take appropriate action before they become larger, more complicated problems. The training our human resource counselors have received enables them to mediate all types of conflicts, not just those related to possible discrimination claims. Now all of our employees are aware that they have a plausible avenue to pursue through our office of human resources if they have a problem, where they will receive guidance and possible options to consider. I am please at how well this new program has been accepted and embraced by the workforce.

Recruitment and Diversity

One of our biggest challenges in recent years is the issue of recruiting. The problems associated with the recruitment and retention of a qualified, diverse workforce of police officers are not unique to the New York State Police and have become a primary focus of police agencies across the country. Fortunately for us, Superintendent McMahon had the vision to recognize this problem early, during the formation of the Office of Human Resources, so we have placed a great deal of focus on strategic interventions to address this issue.

The importance and value of a diverse workforce are well recognized in virtually every business and industry; however, given the nature of police work, it may be even more critical for law enforcement. For a police agency to be truly effective, it must represent the public it serves. Perhaps the biggest benefit is the added trust the public feels in dealing with an officer who looks like them, speaks like them, and understands their culture.

The recruitment of women to the profession of policing remains a unique challenge. Historically, police agencies have been perceived as being white and male, and while that notion has changed over time, policing is still seen by many as a non-traditional occupation for women. Currently, almost 10 percent of our sworn officers are female, a relatively high percentage for state police agencies, which average closer to 5 percent. However, with women representing at least half of the public, it is easy to see that an increase in the share of female troopers would be advantageous.

We decided it was necessary to take affirmative steps to increase the numbers of female applicants for the New York State Police. Recognizing that a change such as this could not be accomplished without a true understanding of the problem, we entered into a partnership with the State University at Albany to conduct a study called "Improving the Recruitment of Women in Law Enforcement." We examined what women are looking for in a career, as well as what women perceive law enforcement to offer, and whether there is a good fit between the two.

We learned that while policing does offer many of the things that women desire in a career, such as good salary and benefits, job security, and the opportunity for job enrichment, there are still commonly held misperceptions about policing, perhaps fueled by the media, which often portray an inaccurate sense of what police officers do on a day-to-day basis.

Based on information gleaned from this study, we asked ourselves, Do we need to market our occupation better so that we can make people aware that policing might actually be an occupation they're interested in? We then refocused a large part of our recruitment campaign to tie into the results of the study. One thing we learned was that while salary was important, equally important to women in a career were job enrichment and variety, and family-friendly policies. We tried to highlight many of the compatible characteristics offered by the New York State Police to demonstrate that a career in policing could be a good career match for females.

Recruitment Challenges

Given the competitive job market, it's certainly more difficult to recruit police officers today than it used to be. Specifically, the recruitment and retention of police officers remain major issues for police agencies across the country. I currently serve as the co-chair of the Diversity Coordinating Panel for the IACP (International Association of Chiefs of Police). This panel was formed to identify and deal with issues relating to diversity in policing, so recruitment is a primary focus of our panel. I hear repeatedly that recruitment of police officers is difficult, and in some agencies, they are unable to find anyone to fill even one open position.

Many factors contribute to this challenge, but I believe that one of the most important ones is our changing workforce. It is clear that the youth of today value different things than those of past generations. Many of our more senior officers ask why we have to recruit and entice young people to join our organization, as no one did that for them. We need to be cognizant that there are, in fact, generational differences, and if we want to remain competitive, we must recognize this dynamic and adjust where appropriate.

We recently conducted a training session for all of the recruiters and our supervisors, designed to help them understand the differences among the generations, particularly the newest addition to the workforce, those representing Generation Y. It was extremely valuable and well received, as it enabled people to understand why their employees did not always act the way we might expect them to. The attendees learned to think outside the traditional ways of doing things and realized that to get the most out of your people, you often need to be willing make adjustments in how you deal with them.

HR's Impact on Our Mission

The mission of the New York State Police is to serve, protect, and defend the people while preserving the rights and dignity of all, a very broad police mission. For police agencies, this means that our core mission is to serve the public. What had been missing was a recognition that we also need to pay attention to our employees, because a happier and more satisfied employee will be a more productive employee and will remain with the agency longer.

The formation of the Office of Human Resources brought focus to that issue and demonstrated that taking care of our employees is consistent with our mission. We've been able to develop a number of programs that we didn't have before, such as job share programs for our civilian employees and an enhancement of our Employee Assistance Program (EAP) for all employees. We have a number of both sworn and civilian employees who have recently been, or currently are, deployed to serve our country overseas. That may mean that one day they are fighting in a war, and then the next day they are back on the road serving as a trooper. Our EAP staff worked to develop a strategy for debriefing our military personnel when they return and assisting them with readjustment issues. This is a fairly new direction for us; I don't think that would have happened ten years ago.

Today our Office of Human Resources is viewed by many as the "touchy-feely" office—and while that isn't consistent with the image police have traditionally had, it has been recognized as a valuable addition to the agency, and a mechanism to address problems that may not have been easily addressed in the past.

Impact of Social Trends

The role of human resources departments is ever-changing, as it is our job to respond to issues as they arise and trends within society that may affect our employees. Currently, a big issue that companies face is the price of gasoline and the struggling economy. Many companies and agencies are responding by allowing their employees the option of working a four-day work week, not only to save money for their employees, but also to save money for the company.

The issue of quality of life for police officers has recently become a primary focus for police unions, and while most police agencies must provide continual 24/7 coverage to their citizens, it is possible to balance quality of life issues with operational mandates. Within the New York State Police, we recently negotiated with the unions a modified work schedule that allows troopers to work a twelve-hour day, reporting for duty only seven out of every fourteen days. This provides the officer with a more regular, predictable schedule and allows them to perform the job and still meet the demands of childcare and home life.

Employee Buy-In and Perception

To establish buy-in of any new initiative, it is important to know the perception of the employees. Sometimes I see a tendency for our managers or supervisors to dictate what the issue is—to tell employees, "This is the problem." To gain a real understanding of the complexities of a particular issue, you need to go to the grassroots and find out how the employees perceive it, which may be entirely different from what management thinks. It's important to get their input and make them part of the strategy and part of the solution—this is how you earn their buy-in.

In establishing our new EEO process, we recognized that we were placing a great deal of responsibility on the shoulders of the HR counselors to make the process work, so it was critical to ensure their buy-in and support. One thing that has been very effective is that our human resources counselors are assigned to locations throughout the state, making them readily accessible to employees within their troops and details. However, that makes it more difficult for staff from the Office of Human Resources to remain in contact with them and make them feel like a part, or an extension of the office.

To deal with this potential problem, members of the human resources staff travel to each troop yearly and conduct meetings with all of the human resources counselors and all of the troop supervisors at the management level. This face-to-face contact enables us to discuss any important human resources initiatives and allows for direct input from our people. It is amazing how a small thing like this empowers them and makes them feel their opinion is valued and important to the agency. This has further enhanced their support of the human resources program and the likelihood that they will serve as "ambassadors" for the office. This has been especially useful when there is a change in policy for the organization.

For example, we recently changed our maternity policy, making it much more worker-friendly and allowing our pregnant members to continue working longer into their pregnancies. Though positive for the membership, as well as the agency, this change affected procedures that had been in place, so there were many questions as to the logistics of how it would work. We used these troop meetings as an opportunity to explain it to both human resources counselors, who would deal with our affected employees, and management personnel, who would have the responsibility to implement the procedures. This also served to ensure that everyone received the same message and that we could address any problems that might arise immediately.

As deputy superintendent, Colonel Deborah J. Campbell holds the distinction of being the highest-ranking female in the eighty-nine-year history of the New York State Police and serves in the fourth-highest-ranking position in the agency. She currently serves as a liaison between the New York State Police and the New York State Division of Criminal Justice Services and is responsible for coordination of efforts and enhanced communication between the two agencies. Previously, she was in charge of the division's Office of Human Resources, including EEO investigations, recruitment, promotional examinations, the Employee Assistance Program, and personnel.

In 2000, Col. Campbell effectuated a research study titled "Improving the Recruitment of Women in Policing: An Investigation of Women's Attitudes and Job Preferences," results of which have been presented nationally and have been instrumental in significantly increasing the number of female applicants for the New York State Police. She also coauthored an article appearing in the May 2002 edition of Law and Order magazine titled "Recruiting Women Police Officers" and continues to play an active role in improving the recruitment efforts of the New York State Police. In 2005, Col. Campbell was presented with the National Center for Women & Policing's Lifetime Achievement Award for the work she has done in improving the recruitment of women to policing.

In addition, Col. Campbell is an active member of several outside organizations, including the National Center for Women & Policing, the International Association of Chiefs of Police, the New York State Chiefs of Police Association, and the New York State Women's Advisory Counsel to the Governor. She currently serves in the position of secretary/treasurer for the State Provincial Division of the IACP, and serves as co-chair of the recently formed IACP Diversity Coordinating Panel, a group tasked with working to enhance the diversity of law enforcement agencies.

Col. Campbell currently resides in Hillsdale, New York, with her husband and two children.

Dedication: *I would like to dedicate this chapter to my father, Martin Tuczinski, who passed away recently after a battle with cancer. My dad was a constant source of inspiration for me and taught me that I could do anything I put my mind to. He encouraged and supported my decision to join the New York State Police, reminding me never to be discouraged by barriers, either real or perceived.*

Developing Hiring Strategies to Promote Growth

Jennifer Fox Crisp
Chief Recruiting Officer
King & Spalding LLP

ASPATORE

Hiring Strategy

I oversee the hiring of lawyers into the firm at all levels, in all offices. I work with our partners to develop hiring strategies that promote our growth strategy. In my opinion, a smart recruiting strategy is thoughtful and targeted—and, most importantly, supports the organization's strategic priorities. So our strategy is to hire the lawyers who have the practice expertise to serve our clients' needs and the combination of IQ and EQ necessary to deliver client service in a manner that is consistent with our culture and expectations.

Recent Changes

In 2005 and 2006, the law firm undertook a strategic review of our practice and our performance in the context of the broader legal market. We then developed a firm-wide strategic plan, which identifies our growth, practice, and industry sector priorities and opportunities going forward. Specifically, we decided to build on our historical strengths. The strategic priorities have provided a specific framework against which to evaluate all hiring decisions, particularly at the most senior levels. We have looked to lateral partner acquisition and expansion into new geographies as a means to further the goals of the strategic plan—demonstrating a greater willingness to bring in people outside the law firm people who have that expertise or are located in the places that our clients need us to be located.

At the other end of the hiring spectrum, the market for new lawyers (those just finishing law school) is changing. Associate pay increases and rate sensitivity from clients is making the new lawyer market more competitive than it has been since 2000. In fact, it is similar to the one found in the early 1990s. Firms are bringing in fewer lawyers, allowing them to be more selective about whom they choose to join the practice.

Measuring Success

We are succeeding every day. In the last eighteen months, we have opened eight offices on three continents, with every office connected in multiple ways to the strategic priorities of the law firm. We have found the right people to open offices, work with our clients, and further our firm strategy.

Like any business, we measure success according to our ability to grow the firm profitably. We will evaluate whether our growth in terms of people and geography results in new client opportunities, e.g., whether the hiring of a new lawyer results in new clients or additional work from current firm clients.

On the people side, I believe that one measure of success is retention, i.e., whether the new hires stay at the firm over the long haul. Cultural integration is another way to measure success. In terms of talent and leadership development, we have refined our on-boarding and integration processes, important ways to drive cultural integration and retention. We want the lawyers we have brought in to identify themselves as King & Spalding lawyers—not with former firm members.

Hiring Process

I am the head of the recruiting department, which comprises thirteen professionals. Recruiting is responsible for lawyer hiring (but not staff hiring, which is handled by human resources). We work closely with the designated hiring partners, practice group leaders, and office managing partners. I also work with our director of strategic projects and director of professional development in developing and executing hiring strategies.

In terms of process, we have defined recruiting processes that we follow when hiring summer associates, lateral associates, and lateral partners. Certain steps must be taken, regardless of whether we are hiring a health care lawyer, a transactional lawyer, or a tort litigator. Our local recruiting managers in each office and their teams handle summer associate and lateral associate hiring, while our assistant director of recruiting is the lead for lateral partner hiring across the firm. By centralizing administrative responsibility for the more intense and highly confidential lateral partner hiring process, we found a smart way to handle growth across offices. It is efficient and effective to have a single point of contact working with me, the lateral partner committee, the policy committee, and the practice group leaders as we engage in hiring at senior levels.

Researching Recruiting Strategies

A good practice is always to look back at what we have done in the past to identify ways to leverage our successes and learn from our disappointments.

As any smart business does, we look to the leading industry and non-industry practices to see what we can learn to improve our hiring approach and client service delivery. We evaluate the strategies and relative successes of other law firms, as well as other professional services firms, e.g., Big Four accounting firms and management consulting firms. We look at the accounting and consulting firms because they, too, are knowledge-intensive businesses, and all knowledge-intensive businesses are challenged to attract and retain highly mobile top talent. In terms of other law firms, from time to time, there are articles about other firms' growth strategies and seminars to attend, which provide an opportunity to compare notes. However, because of the private nature of a partnership, they frequently do not provide a significant amount of data.

Unlike a company that sells a product, we cannot as easily "market-test" a new offering through a limited focus group introduction. On the other hand, before opening a new office, we certainly do research by talking to our clients to make sure that our presence in a certain location and our ability to offer a certain service are attractive to them—and that they will be inclined to hire us. That kind of research is helpful in informing our growth decisions.

For example, we opened our Washington office because the Coca-Cola Company requested our presence on the ground there; similarly, we opened in Houston because of a request from Chevron. We are not in the "flag-planting" mode in expansion, unlike other firms that gobble up boutique or smaller firms or even mid-size firms to be able to say that they have a global footprint. That is not how we do it. We don't think an integrated approach furthers our strategy. For our first 118 years, we opened only four offices outside of Atlanta to meet our client needs.

Future Growth Strategy

In the future, we will continue building the expertise that our clients demand by hiring the top players in the industry. We want the best and the brightest in terms of subject matter expertise. A full 100 percent of my budget goes to talent acquisition. I know my hiring practices are successful when, two years from now, I can say that I have hired the best in the industries that we are targeting, built significant capability in key practice areas, and expanded our footprint by bringing in the right people who are serving clients well and fit into the culture.

Client Service Orientation

Unlike companies that deliver a tangible product to the marketplace, lawyers deliver wisdom and intellectual insight to our clients. Our assets are our people, and they walk out of the door each evening. The competition for top-notch lawyers is fierce, and job mobility is high. To recruit and retain in a knowledge-intensive environment means that ensuring a match between the firm's expectations of our lawyers and the lawyer's expectations of the workplace is essential. We are a service business, so we must recruit highly qualified talent who have as a focus a client-service orientation. Being smart may get you in the door for an interview—being both high-performing and collegial will get you hired.

As a firm, we have articulated Client Service Principles—that is, what we expect of our lawyers in their service delivery. Our Client Service Principles grew out of feedback from our clients who were willing to take the time to describe what they value about engaging the firm and why they continue to do so. For potential hires who do not demonstrate the qualities embodied by the Client Service Principles, this firm is not the place for them. In an article published in *Smart Business* magazine, our chairman has said, "I'm a big believer that good is the enemy of the great. Good is not good enough. You have to have great people—and to do that, you have to insist on greatness and have high standards across the board." We believe in being upfront during the interview process about our high standards.

Similarly, our lawyers are supported by our able non-lawyer staff. Over the past five years we have implemented our Service Excellence Initiative (SEI) to promote a focus on client service on the staff side, as well. SEI's mission statement is simple: "We listen to, anticipate, and exceed our internal clients' needs through team work, initiative, and dedication to quality." It closely parallels the traits we value in our lawyers. We have developed ten SEI Service Standards to which all staff members are held accountable. The SEI program is administered through the human resources department.

Growing Your Company: The Role of Recruiting in Firm Expansion

Recent Growth: Expansion versus Acquisition

While we have not recently undertaken a merger or acquisition of another law firm, in the past eighteen months, we have acquired individual lawyers and groups of lawyers from other law firms whose expertise furthers our strategic plan, as well as opened new offices across the world. We have hired groups and individual lateral partners for existing offices to build capabilities. For example, in May 2008 six health care partners and nine associates left a competitor to join our Washington and Houston offices—a result of our identification of health care as a strategic initiative for the firm.

Since January 2007, we have opened eight offices on three continents and populated them with a mix of current firm lawyers who have relocated, new individual lateral partners, and groups of lateral partners, associates, and staff. This is not necessarily the typical approach of law firm growth. As noted above, many firms simply choose to bolt on practices and offices to an existing firm via acquisition to expand their global and practice reach, not to mention their client base. We do not believe this bolt-on approach yields what we believe is important in terms of fit and successful integration. In fact, our typical approach to opening new offices involves current firm lawyers relocating to a new office to help launch the office; they are culture carriers.

We undertook this approach when opening offices in Washington, D.C., Houston, London, Dubai, and Abu Dhabi. We believe it is important to explain our expansion consistently in the context of our strategic priorities. Our expansion into the Middle East comes as a direct result of our focus on the energy sector and our internationally recognized Islamic finance practice. Our addition of two intellectual property partners and nine associates to help open the Silicon Valley office in January 2008 resulted from our identification of patent litigation as a strategic priority. We believe it is important to communicate not only what happened, but also why it makes sense for the firm.

Opening New Offices

We identified patent litigation as a strategic initiative and recognized that to be at the top of the game, it was important to have a presence in California to serve the high-tech and life sciences clients located there. The practice group leader of the intellectual property practice, someone who began his career as a summer associate at the firm, volunteered to relocate to open our offices in Northern California, bringing more than twelve years of intellectual property expertise and immersion in firm culture with him.

Our Silicon Valley office opened in February 2008 and now includes fourteen lawyers with expertise in patent litigation, patent prosecution, and the FDA (U.S. Food and Drug Administration). This builds on expansion of our intellectual property capabilities through our hiring thirteen partners in Atlanta, Houston, New York, and Washington over the past eighteen months.

Lateral Hiring

Recruiting, human resources, and our professional development department play a number of key roles during these group acquisitions, including facilitating the interview and due diligence process, on-boarding, and transition/integration planning. The firm has devoted significant energy and resources to structuring and standardizing the lateral hiring process to improve the probability that we are making the right hires and that the people we hire choose to stay and embrace firm culture.

For example, we have developed a comprehensive pre-hire diligence checklist, which ensures not only that we are making good decisions based on full information pre-hire, but also that we communicate the productivity expectations to new potential partners prior to their joining the firm so as to eliminate surprises once they have arrived. We developed a transition manual that we give to new partners prior to their arrival to facilitate the early integration process, and we require a three-month integration plan to be submitted along with any proposal to hire a new partner.

Attracting Talent

Our method of growth has made us more attractive to the top laterals because they know where the firm is going and how they will fit in. By having articulated to ourselves where we are going, we have created an incredible tool with which to attract top candidates. Our strategy is to hire and expand deliberately in the areas that we think build on current strengths and leverage current client relationships and market opportunities. We are not interested in basic acquisitions to simply add lawyer headcount. We prefer to be more deliberate.

Challenges of Growth

We are in a recognized and focused growth mode, which necessitated our developing a standardized partner hiring process. We want to make sure that we do the right amount of due diligence on our hires and effectively sell them on the firm. This has placed greater responsibility on what we call "sponsoring partners"—partners who have identified individuals or groups they wish to hire. We ask sponsoring partners to take responsibility for shepherding the candidates through the hiring process and ensure their integration into the firm. Once a lateral partner joins us, he or she is immediately treated as a partner in the firm.

International Integration

Not unique to us, but one of the challenges of integrating partners in international locations is actually getting them all together at one time. Gathering the partnership together for a videoconference when you have offices reaching from Dubai to San Francisco can be a challenge.

At this point, all of our lawyers speak English, usually as well as other languages, so once we overcome the distance barrier, there is no language barrier. In the Middle East, our offices are led by an American partner who relocated to Dubai from Houston. He is a real culture carrier, so he sets the tone for our three Middle East offices. Our work in the Middle East is connected with our Islamic finance practice, based in New York, as well as our energy initiative, largely driven from Houston. The Frankfurt office does not have a U.S. partner resident full-time. But our Frankfurt office arose out of our real estate capital markets initiative, and the real estate capital markets are tied to London and New York. This allows the partners to integrate through work, which arguably is the best way to integrate people into a law firm.

Firm Culture

We are in the client service business, and we are in the knowledge business. From a cultural standpoint, we define ourselves as both high performing and collegial. This is not something we made up—it is the feedback we received when we asked about thirty of our top clients to tell us, "What sets King & Spalding apart from other firms?"

The two attributes are not mutually exclusive—in fact, the combination is a powerful one. To embody these characteristics, our people demonstrate a commitment to technical excellence, problem-solving ability, empathy (i.e., standing in the shoes of the client when addressing what appears to be a legal problem but from the client's perspective is a business problem), a solution-oriented approach, and a willingness to check our egos at the door. These cultural markers are universal—they do not vary by office, by department, by practice, or by country. We hire people who as individuals represent the broader cultural norms of high-performance and collegiality. They are also long-standing values, not ones that have recently evolved. I do not think the core values of our high-performance culture have changed. I do think, however, that the globalization of the economy and other market factors have made our leaders more risk-tolerant in terms of expansion than has previously been the case.

In 2006, we undertook a year-long strategic review of our priorities, which included obtaining feedback from our clients. Because of this strategic review, we recognized that we had opportunity to build on the solid foundation of excellence, but to broaden our reach to new clients and in new locations. We have deliberately pursued our expansion objectives using the strategy as the guiding principle. Since January 2007, the firm has opened eight new offices on three continents; in our first 118 years of existence, the firm added only four offices outside of the original Atlanta base.

Cultural Integration

We are up front about our culture during the hiring process. Organizationally many of our practice groups span multiple offices. How we serve our clients does not vary based on where you are located or what sort of law you practice. Cultural integration of new hires at all levels of the firm, from senior partners to non-lawyer staff, is a priority and, we believe, a measure of our success.

We execute these integration plans in a number of ways, from sending new hires to established offices to "shadow" their peers in these offices on the administrative side to formal training sessions for new and lateral associates to the development of formal integration plans for new partner hires. Identifying integration as a discrete goal, as opposed to simply assuming that it will happen over time, and recognizing that true integration expands far beyond day one orientation is a departure from previous practices. Our goal has not changed, and it is straightforward; we want happy, productive lawyers and staff and want to do whatever is necessary to achieve this.

Merger and Acquisition Practices

Consolidation among law firms via merger and acquisition has been increasing in recent years. Globalization of clients' businesses in part drives the desire for law firms to expand their geographic and practice expertise such that they can be the trusted advisers to clients wherever they have a need. Also, mergers or acquisitions can benefit a firm tremendously where clients and practices are complementary but conflicts of interest are minimal. Through our expansion approach, we benefit not only by gaining the expertise of new lawyers to serve our clients and by the addition of new clients, but also by learning from them about some of the leading practices that their prior firms had used.

There are those who expect that law firms will go the way of the Big Four (formerly Big Five, formerly Big Eight) accounting firms, with only a few mega-firms standing at the end. I believe that ethics rules surrounding conflicts of interest will likely prevent that sort of consolidation in the industry, but I do expect that we will see more and more firms undertaking merger and/or acquisition activity.

Measuring Success

While our expansion is relatively recent in the context of our more than one hundred-year history, I believe we will measure the success of our growth activity according to several benchmarks. First and foremost is client satisfaction. We will also measure additional client business achieved through cross-selling, either via introduction of a new partner's clients to others in the law firm or introduction of the new partner to current clients. Success can also be measured by the cultural integration of new hires, their length of service, i.e., retention, and the level of our activity in our new offices, e.g., our expansion into the Middle East.

Jennifer Fox Crisp joined King & Spalding as chief recruiting officer in August 2004. She is responsible for development and execution of attorney recruitment strategy for the entire firm.

Ms. Crisp is an attorney with expertise in developing and implementing organizational effectiveness, recruiting and retention, and talent management strategies for organizations seeking to optimize human capital.

Prior to joining King & Spalding, Ms. Crisp was a senior manager at Deloitte Consulting in the human capital practice. Her consulting experience encompassed the broad range of highly integrated activities designed to ensure that people strategies reflect and reinforce business strategies throughout the employee lifecycle.

Ms. Crisp is a graduate of the University of Pennsylvania Law School and Duke University.

Responding to Evolving Market Conditions with a Flexible HR Strategy

Jodie Garfinkel

Director, Professional Personnel and Attorney Development

Vaughn Burke

Director, Human Resources

Skadden, Arps, Slate, Meagher & Flom LLP

ASPATORE

Introduction and Company Background

Jodie Garfinkel is the director of professional personnel and attorney development, and Vaughn Burke is the director of human resources for Skadden, Arps, Slate, Meagher & Flom LLP. Skadden divides its human resources functions into three groups: attorneys, legal assistants, and support staff. Mr. Burke is responsible for human resources administration for support staff, including recruitment, training and development, performance management, policy and procedure documentation, and administration and separation. Ms. Garfinkel is responsible for all aspects of human resources administration, except recruitment, for attorneys.

Skadden is unique among top-tier U.S.-based firms in that it was established just sixty years ago. But since its founding in 1948, the firm has experienced tremendous growth, both domestically and internationally. Today it is the largest U.S. firm, in terms of revenue, and has about 2,000 attorneys in twenty-four offices around the world. That kind of rapid growth has obvious implications for the firm's HR strategies, requiring flexibility toward new approaches coupled with maintaining the best practices that helped the firm achieve its remarkable success.

Components of a Successful HR Strategy

Any successful HR strategy has to be flexible because the candidate population, the needs of the firm, and industry conditions all change rapidly and simultaneously. Like all components of successful law firm management, HR strategy must be able to anticipate, adapt to, and respond to evolving market conditions. So a recurring theme for us is this: A critical part of HR is to understand both our employees and the firm—and find the intersection where the skills and the interests of our employees match the needs of the firm. In other words, how can we leverage the talents, skills, and interests of our employees in the best and most productive way possible?

Typically, in the context of law firms, we would insert a caveat that HR considerations diverge for attorneys and support staff. But this key consideration—which shapes and influences all of our strategies—applies equally to both groups.

The evolving nature of the legal industry necessitates that a successful HR strategy also be forward thinking. While we obviously must tackle situations in the here and now, we also strive to anticipate where things are headed so that we will be prepared for unexpected, as well as expected, changes. This includes generational changes in the workforce. The needs and expectations of law school students joining us as associates today, for example, are dramatically different from those who are now senior partners at the firm. The Skadden experience has taught us, if nothing else, that the law firm of tomorrow will look very different from the law firm we see today.

Shifts in Strategy

Because the theme of our overall HR strategy encompasses the concept of change, as long as we make that concept our guiding principle, by definition our strategies will constantly evolve. While the firm's overarching priorities have remained consistent, the needs of our attorneys, our clients, and our staff have certainly changed over time, and we try to be responsive to those needs.

One of the things that have helped us be responsive is that today's employees are much more willing to offer feedback about their roles and how the firm's policies and procedures affect them. Previous generations of personnel would grin and bear it—just accepting what their employers had to offer. As time passed, however, the idea of gauging employee responses and reactions and leveraging them as a resource has become increasingly important, and in turn, employees have become more willing to deliver constructive feedback.

Recent HR Strategies at Skadden

We are constantly working on numerous HR initiatives at Skadden. For the past several years, our focus has become much more global. We started out as a New York firm and branched out in the United States, but our more recent growth and development have been international. We have had to stretch what was and is very much a one-firm philosophy to encompass a much broader population. That has been one of the biggest adjustments we've had to make and think about as we move forward.

Some of what was critical to the success of our initiatives—and continues to be critical in any initiative—is obvious, such as garnering support from the firm's top leadership and achieving buy-in and consensus from the various constituencies. Recognizing that these things can help ensure success, we look to gather the necessary support before we actually roll out new programs.

Best Practices: Marrying Employee and Business Needs

Our best practices have involved carefully reviewing what our employees need in terms of skills, interests, and opportunities for development, and what our clients need, and then marrying the two.

Our attorney satisfaction surveys and support staff questionnaires led us to identify new performance management tools to help us stimulate dialogues between employees and managers, associates and partners. In these dialogues we can discover where an employee has opportunities for improvement, and where he or she may have skills that we are not tapping into that can be used to better service our clients.

Legal versus Corporate Environments

It is important to note distinctions between the legal industry and corporate environments. In terms of best practices, privately owned professional service firms—of which law firms are one type—have different drivers than publicly traded companies do. In a corporate environment you must often appeal to the public, because those are your customers and your shareholders. In a professional service organization, particularly a partnership, the partners make up the ownership structure. They, rather than shareholders looking in from outside the company, set the direction for the firm and are key to the development and maintenance of the culture. This creates a different dynamic from the corporate environment that cannot be overstated.

Rather than being a detriment, however, we find that this inward-looking structure provides an opportunity and an advantage. The popular perception is that public companies are marching to a predefined beat or meeting predetermined standards of performance that are set collectively, but generally outside the organization. Shareholders vote with their dollars and their feet and, by their actions, determine a company's strategic course.

A private company, on the other hand, can set its own course and leverage employees and their talents to move the company in a desired direction without necessarily having to rely on, or respond to, externally established paradigms. The marketplace, of course, will always have an impact on a law firm's business, as well, because law firms are not insulated from general economic and business conditions. But a partnership can itself determine the best way to anticipate and respond to changing economics without the pressures of shareholders.

Budgeting Issues

It is difficult to compare our spending breakdowns to other law firms because law firm finances are closely held. Based on programming costs and contact with industry counterparts, we believe we are far ahead of the pack in terms of the quality, quantity, and variety of training and development opportunities we provide.

It is also perhaps unusual in the law firm environment that our people—lawyers and staff—are engaged in the training process from the minute they walk through the door, and training continues throughout an individual's career at Skadden.

Essential Research

Despite recognizing we are quite different from public companies, we do look outside the legal field to evaluate best practices in other industries, in organizations both similar to and different from ours. This kind of research requires vision and imagination to apply strategies from outside our sphere of experience within our environment.

We are not comfortable with the status quo; that is simply not part of Skadden's DNA. So an attitude of, "This is the way it has always been done, so this is the way we'll do it going forward," does not suit us. Instead, our approach has always been, "Let's take a fresh look and reassess the situation," and "Let's continue to look at the facts and needs as they evolve, in addition to what experience has taught us, and then decide how to proceed."

Top Down and Bottom Up: 360 Degrees of Support

While it is always important to have top-down support in implementing new strategies, buy-in is needed from the bottom up, as well. In some ways you want 360 degrees of support. To that end, we match mentors to new employees to make sure there is someone an employee can go to who is on a similar career path or at a similar level of development.

We also educate our partners and managers about what people need to be fully functioning. Certainly staff in each of our departments is charged with making sure not only that assignments are being made, but that there is follow-through and a high level of engagement on all fronts. The only way a new initiative can be successfully implemented is if everyone understands what his or her role is in the process and embraces that role.

Involving Staff and Attorneys

The underlying theme to any good implementation is that the initiative be driven by a collaborative approach. We use surveys and otherwise elicit feedback to involve both the support staff and the attorneys in each process.

From a support staff perspective, we recently conducted a broad reassessment of our HR strategies. We looked carefully at how we were managing performance: how we were setting expectations, how we were giving feedback about how those expectations were being met, how we were communicating where there were opportunities for improvement, and how we were targeting training and development.

We began by examining some external best practices and then looking at our firm through internal questionnaires. We sent questionnaires to our staff, then collected the feedback and used an outside consultant to help us analyze what the results were actually telling us, before using that feedback to determine our next steps in the change. We found that process was invaluable because not only did we get useful feedback from people on the front line who were able to tell us how to better manage our resources, but it also allowed those people to feel connected to the change process, which then makes its implementation much easier.

On the attorney side, it is a similar story. We conducted a survey on a full range of topics to assess the priorities of the workforce as it was changing, as the demands were changing, and as technology was changing. That then allowed us to set priorities based on the realities of the attorney experience.

Leveraging Technology

Enhanced technological capabilities have provided a number of different resources, such as the surveys previously discussed. In that example, we were able to slice and dice data in ways that otherwise would have been quite difficult. We have found other ways to take advantage of technological know-how. Using technology to maintain databases, for example, frees employees to devote time and energy to higher-level tasks than data management and updating records. For example, we used to have a staff member who devoted significant time to updating employee addresses and phone numbers. Now, employees can just go online through a secure access and update information themselves. This frees the person who might otherwise have been charged with doing what was a pretty basic task—creating a resource that can be used for a higher level of work and shifting an employee to more challenging, and more rewarding, tasks.

Technology is also valuable in training. We utilize it to support a wide variety of activities, from computer-based programs to tracking and using training to identify areas that people need to develop, from data management, and even to policy administration. As technology develops, it allows us to bypass those more mundane tasks to use our employees' talent on more creative endeavors.

Furthermore, technology has greatly supported our efforts at collaboration. With nearly 6,000 employees, including 2,000 attorneys, spread across five continents, technology enables attorneys and staff to engage in a kind of virtual dialogue, using information speedily conveyed and accessed.

Measuring Success

By definition, as a professional services organization, we strive to provide the highest level of service. This is amplified at Skadden because it is on superior client service that we stake our reputation and strive to distinguish ourselves from other legal service providers. Therefore, when we define success, we are measuring whether we were actually able to offer a higher level of service, and whether that service leads to greater levels of engagement from our clients. We can also measure our success internally, based on the retention of our key contributors and top performers; we want to make sure they are engaged and satisfied, and we are not losing them to competitors.

Aside from retention and employee satisfaction, we can also benchmark a strategy's effectiveness by looking at how productively people are working. By productive, we do not mean in the sense of producing widgets; we define productivity as maintaining the highest quality work product.

Upcoming Trends and Strategies

Over the next twelve months and beyond, we will continue to refine and focus on the strategies and tactics currently commanding our attention. One of our short-term initiatives is looking at how we recruit candidates to make sure that someone offered a position is provided with as much information as possible during the interview process, allowing the candidate to make an appropriate decision about whether this is the right place for him or her. Skadden is a demanding, high-performance environment with a lot of activity, and high expectations are placed on employees. We want to make sure that when we bring people in, they are ready for and willing to meet the challenges they will face. In addition, we are strengthening our orientation process, so that during an employee's first six months, there will be a more hands-on interaction among employees, managers, and mentors. This should further ensure that job expectations are clearly defined and our new employees receive the support they need to succeed.

On the attorney side, career development is an area of more recent focus. Our strategy is not simply checking how people are doing against the current standards and circumstances, but also trying to reach the next level by planning and ensuring that attorneys remain engaged and understand what is expected of them. As part of the HR function, it is important that we take a proactive role, as opposed to a merely reactive one, in what happens with people and their careers. We want to anticipate the needs of our attorneys so we can better assure their success, rather than just react to problem situations.

Trends within the legal industry also will affect our HR strategies, and one of the most challenging trends is the increased interest in telecommuting. We think that the idea of working outside the office will become more and more important, and we therefore need to address how to accommodate employees working remotely. How do you manage people who are working remotely? How can you make sure they get what they need to do the job? How are you able to assess whether they perform appropriately? These are just a few of the questions that will need to be addressed.

Other important issues that will have an impact on HR practices in the future include the concept of work/life balance, which continues to be a challenge, and especially so in an environment in which an imperative for outstanding client service demands that employees be ready whenever and wherever the clients' needs take them.

Diversity is another key concern: there has been a tremendous inward review of diversity within the legal profession and a consideration of how it compares internally with the corporate world. Clients also recognize this issue as one we need to collaborate on, which is another driver. Recently Skadden joined with The City College of New York to create a unique honors program for pre-law students, with the objective of recruiting talented students from diverse backgrounds to a career in law.

Jodie Garfinkel is the director of professional personnel and attorney development at Skadden, Arps, Slate, Meagher & Flom, a global law firm with more than 2,000 attorneys and twenty-four offices. She has been with the firm since 1984, first serving as the manager of associate development. As one of the first attorney development professionals at a major firm, Ms. Garfinkel considers Skadden Arps a true leader in recognizing the value of professional administration, particularly in its support of attorney development.

Ms. Garfinkel's professional responsibilities include training and development, evaluations and performance reviews, salary administration, work/life programming, foreign associate programming, and management of personnel administration. Prior to joining Skadden Arps, Ms. Garfinkel was the recruiting coordinator and then the associate director of placement at New York University School of Law.

Ms. Garfinkel holds a Master of Arts degree in counseling from New York University. She graduated from Barnard College, magna cum laude, with a Bachelor of Arts in psychology.

Vaughn Burke is the director of human resources at Skadden, Arps, Slate, Meagher & Flom LLP. He is responsible for human resources administration for support staff, including recruitment, training and development, performance management, and policy administration.

Mr. Burke has been with Skadden since October of 1993. He first joined as a legal assistant case manager, and then became a manager in the finance department, subsequently moving to human resources. Having performed varied roles during his fifteen years with Skadden, Mr. Burke recognizes the importance of collaboration in fostering a productive work environment that is ready and able to deal with the opportunities and challenges that a changing workforce presents.

Mr. Burke graduated from Princeton University in 1986 with a Bachelor of Arts degree in molecular biology.

Better Recruiting Strategies Result in Better Business Practices

Don Davis

Senior Vice President, Human Resources
Headway Corporate Resources

ASPATORE

A Different Type of HR

As the senior vice president of human resources (HR), I deal with all the HR functions for our temporary and internal staff. We partner with other companies to develop an overall approach to staffing to meet their individual needs. We'll become the HR department and manage HR strategy for our partner companies while they focus on their core areas of expertise.

For example, one of our clients does social research studies. The studies can last from a couple of months to a couple of years, depending on the subject and method of collection. We work with them to develop and supply them with interviewers who can go from one project to another. We try to keep people so that the knowledge stays within the company. We stay in touch with the interviewers so that when new projects arise, they are available.

Successful Strategy

The creation of a successful business strategy, whether for HR, finance, or marketing, is the same. You first have to determine what you want to accomplish. Once that is decided, you must figure out the best way to reach that goal. After you develop a process, you need to stick with it and follow through until you attain your ultimate goal.

Recent Changes in HR Strategies

In the HR industry in general we're developing more partnerships. In the past, a client called and requested one person to fill one particular position whenever a vacancy occurred. Many companies looked at staffing as a way to fill in gaps. In the past five years, that one-off relationship has turned into a partnership. We now work with companies more often on a project basis, helping them find candidates for certain areas on a regular basis. We take care of all the staffing, allowing the partner company to focus on the goals they need to accomplish for their business.

Measuring Success

Headway has developed strategies as a way to sell the business. We are able to discuss our projects and our success stories as a way to sell our strategy and our business. We are able to measure that success in small ways. Do our employees stay on through their project? Did the clients meet their goals? Will the client use us again for their next project?

Best Practices

The best practice in terms of selling staffing is to listen to the client. We are not a large staffing company. We're more like a boutique staffing company. One of our best practices is not to impose something that we already have in place for one client and offer it as the answer to a problem for a different client. We prefer to listen to the needs of each individual client and be flexible enough to meet their goals in an interesting way. It is better to develop something unique for each client than to try to propose one solution to everyone.

Working as a Team

Each client has a dedicated project team to help them achieve their goals. One person makes the initial contact and then hands over the relationship to a project manager. The project is the main point of contact between our company and the client.

Other members of the project team include recruiters, trainers, and various other support staff who work with the employees and maintain the projects as they move forward. Over time, we have included more trainers to help the newly hired employees learn the skills necessary to perform their function.

Service Development

Many of our satisfied customers have increased their business with us. We have one particular client who has been working with us for ten years. The initial partnership was for a small project. They were very happy with the result, and our partnership expanded to include more recruiting and HR.
A few years ago it occurred to us that we could handle other, different types of projects for them and approached them with our ideas. As a result, they have dramatically expanded their business with us. We learned we need to initiate conversations with clients to understand how we can find new ways to meet their growing and changing needs.

Recruiting New Employees

To help meet our recruiting needs, we started a recruiting center. The staff members do not actually meet with the clients. Rather, they receive orders from our recruiters detailing the type of employees we are looking for to fill certain positions. The people in the recruiting center then work to build a database to meet those needs. They source and screen people for each type of position our clients might need, which has resulted in a database of one million people.

Utilizing Technology

The Internet is absolutely essential to our HR strategies. Our recruitment center uses the Internet to help find people and to communicate with people. They use technology 24/7 to find the right people for the right positions. We have good in-house expertise to help develop our recruiters, but we also keep an eye on external sources to stay abreast of what is happening in the world. We do research on how other companies are recruiting, which tools they are using, and whether their tools will help us.

Training Employees

We believe strongly that training will extend our business. The better our employees are at filling the needs of our clients, the more the business grows. As time goes on, we'll continue training our recruiters to find new ways to utilize technology and the Internet.

The vice president of HR must make sure that training is being developed, implemented, and utilized. We want to make sure our recruiters are the absolute best at finding the right people for the right jobs. The director of recruiting and the managers and recruiters at our offices around the country all have a role to play in bringing new technology to the table and making sure we are current in our training practices.

In the future, we hope to have more self-directed training. We do a great deal of one-on-one training, which I think is valuable for the people, but as that recruitment center grows, we will have to standardize and automate some of the training to make that possible.

Building a Budget

My HR budget is rather nebulous. As needs arise, I create proposals to determine what we need to do and how much it will cost. I have never broken down the cost of our training programs. We do try to benchmark how our training programs pay off and how much they increase business for our company. Instead of benchmarking against other companies, we prefer to study our own needs and how well our business goals have benefited from our training programs. I am willing to pay whatever it costs to make us the best in our industry.

Improving Recruiting

When we started out, we spent much of our time building a database of candidates who fit profiles of previous client needs. Now we spend more time focusing on our current business.

We provide direct orders to the recruitment center for the exact types of people we need to fit each client. We have narrowed our search. We no longer ask for someone with general IT knowledge. Now we ask for someone who is expert at certain systems or products. However, our recruiters still need to bring in a broad range of candidates to fill those specialist positions, so we are able to find a number of people who may not be right for that project, but will be great for other projects. They are able to develop relationships and build our database.

Upcoming Industry Trends

Currently, businesses tend to be shy about adding staff to their payroll. As we begin to climb out of our economic downturn, they will be more enthusiastic about finding additional ways to increase production goals. When that happens, we can approach them about new staffing possibilities.

Donald M. Davis is senior vice president of human resources at Headway Corporate Resources. In this role, which he assumed in 1999, Mr. Davis works with operations partners to develop and implement human resources policies and objectives that are aligned with the organization's strategic goals. He determines and recommends employee relations practices necessary to establish a positive employer-employee relationship and promote a high level of employee morale, and identifies legal requirements and government reporting regulations affecting the HR function.

He has previously served as Headway's human resources manager, southeast region, and as benefits administrator.

Headway Corporate Resources is a market leader in the delivery of high-quality recruitment, staffing, outsourcing, and professional development services.

Prior to joining Headway Corporate Resources, Mr. Davis worked in various HR roles at APAC TeleServices Inc., Western Illinois University, and Kelly Temporary Services. He began his HR career in 1986 at Nacel Cultural Exchanges, in Charlottesville, Virginia.

Achieving Business Success through Strategic HR Partnerships

John M. Daniel

Executive Vice President, Human Resources

First Horizon Corporation

ASPATORE

A Successful HR Strategy

A successful human resources strategy is one that is aligned with the business strategy. When I have taken responsibility for HR in large organizations, the first thing I did was to meet top executives and other key leaders. My purpose was to find the answers to some important questions:

- What affects your business?
- What are your key strategies?
- What are the biggest challenges you face?
- What changes in structure, job, and compensation will be required?
- What competencies will your staff need?
- What is your assessment of current leadership and your culture?

Traditionally, HR leaders asked executives to evaluate HR programs and processes in terms of execution success. But a more important assessment is one of effectiveness in helping achieve business goals. In my experience, business leaders don't know what to ask of HR, or they ask for a specific solution that won't resolve the problem. One example of this is management's tendency to see compensation as the source of all problems, like turnover, low morale, and poor productivity. These conclusions are reached because of narrow thinking or flawed research techniques.

HR Organizational Structure

The next step, after developing an understanding of the business, is to ensure the HR organizational structure is right. While HR can provide valuable assistance in ensuring a successful business strategy, we must first get the basics right. The payroll must run on time; jobs must be filled and benefits administered effectively and efficiently. Many companies have used a shared service model as a way of transforming HR.

In an effective shared service model, the HR organization is aligned in a way that best supports its key clients and their needs. Employees need help in resolving basic problems and answering questions. Managers need technical and professional support through services such as recruiting, employee relations, and training. Senior leaders need strategic support on challenges such as leadership development, strategic people planning, and acquisition integration.

Many organizations have designed their HR structure around the three major roles—administrator, professional expert, and strategic partner. Still, many have seen only an incremental increase in value. In my experience, the way to success in introducing the strategic partner model, as illustrated on the next page, is that the HR business partners are completely released of all administrative and operational duties. If the business partners retain responsibility for employee relations, recruiting, or individual problem-solving, they never find time to analyze and resolve organizational problems or resolve obstacles to organizational improvement.

Business Partner Role

Finally, HR leaders need to find the right professional talent to help build and then implement a strategy. HR professionals who combine outstanding relationship skills, the ability to think strategically with reasonable levels of HR experience, and knowledge are rare. But I have seen many times that the right HR business partner can make a huge difference in advancing both the HR strategy and the overall goals of the organization.

Business partners are relationship managers. They are assigned to a large business unit or a group of small ones. They learn the business in detail. How does it make money? What are its distinct competitive advantages? How is it organized and why? What are the skills and backgrounds of those in the workforce? What are the financial and other goals of the business? With the answers to these questions and their own strategic mindset, a business partner can add insights and ideas.

For example, in one organization where I led HR, a new leader became head of one of our largest business units. The HR business partner assigned to the business watched the initial enthusiasm of the promotion deteriorate due to communication breakdowns and poor morale. While initially excited about his new strategy for the business, team members were struggling with execution, and the new leader was disappointed with his new team. The new leader wanted HR's help in replacing his team.

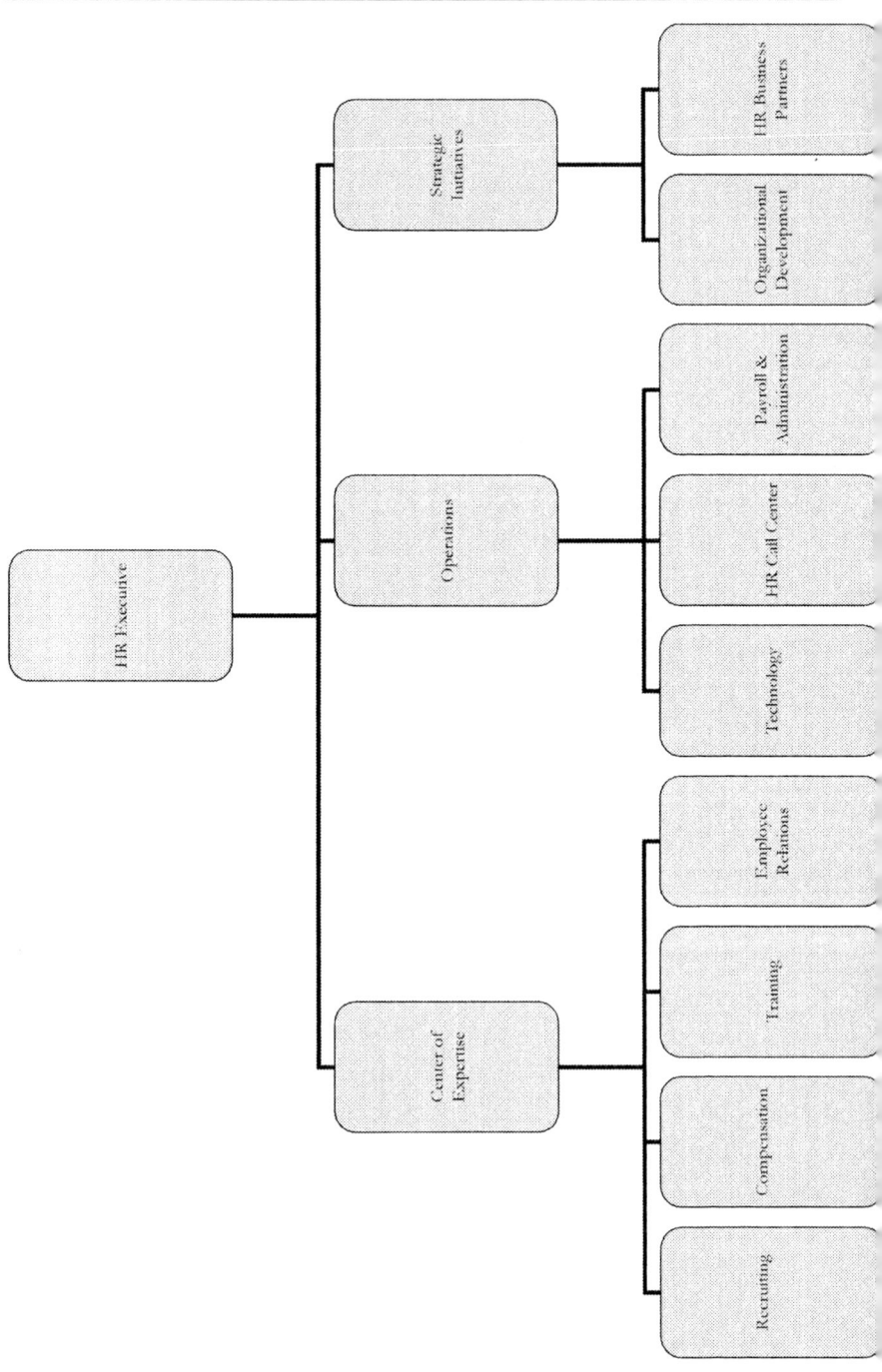

The business partner attended senior staff meetings and met with the executive and team members. She developed a view that the old team was acting in the same way as it had for the former boss. The new leader expected team members to initiate change and challenge his new ideas. But they were accustomed to working for a leader who made all the decisions and didn't appreciate feedback that wasn't positive.

The HR business partner facilitated several working meetings with the team. She led the team through several exercises to build trust, clarify expectations, and change the culture. In a short time, the team was working together more effectively; the leader was pleased; and the performance of the business unit improved.

In review, the business partner didn't act on the first request of the leader to help change out team members. She probed for the root cause of the problem, did research, and took action. The result was not only a satisfied, productive team, but also a better result.

Change Management

With the HR organization repositioned as a strategic partner, many additional opportunities to improve the business emerge. Organizations are constantly going through change, and many times the changes are significant and with system-wide impact. Many senior executives believe that employees will support change initiatives based on a compelling internal business case as laid out by the leader.

Human resources business partners, with an understanding of how employees deal with change and knowledge of change management principles and tactics, know better. In addition to a technology and project plan, human resources business partners help develop change management plans in support of significant change initiatives.

Research shows that around 60 percent of corporate change initiatives fail to meet expectations. The reasons are usually not an incorrect assessment of the problem or opportunity, or even a flawed execution plan. The reasons are often cultural or the ability of affected employees to understand the need for change.

Recently our organization rolled out a companywide transformation initiative. Traditionally the company rolled out major change with an inspiring message from the CEO, kick-off meetings, and a project management plan. Still, change initiatives met with limited success. With this recent initiative, HR was involved at the beginning.

Our first recommendation was to write a case management plan that carried the same importance as the project and technology plans. After the kick-off meeting, HR business partners conducted meetings with all the employees affected by the change. After the CEO and business unit leaders made their business change, affected employees were solicited for their input and ideas. Not only did senior management receive good input, but employees had a chance to discuss and reflect on the needed change as well.

Employees don't change based on their own conclusions. The debrief sessions provided them the opportunity to process the change in a safe, open environment. The sessions were followed with a number of written communications and meetings to keep up the momentum of the project.

Corporate Culture

Sometimes organizational cultures fall out of alignment with business strategies. Human resources is uniquely positioned to identify these situations and develop actions to drive alignment. Our organization recently initiated a culture change initiative because of massive change affecting our banking business.

After the development of our new vision and business strategy, we conducted a cultural assessment using survey tools and focus groups. We developed a clear understanding of our cultural strengths and weaknesses. HR facilitated discussions with senior executives to identify gaps and then developed training and education classes to close the gaps. During the training, leaders spent time reflecting on attributes of the culture that supported our strategy and those that did not. They came to their own conclusions about the need for change and as a result generated excellent recommendations to executive management on needed actions in support of the new strategy.

Human resources, armed with insight about human behavior in organizations and the tools of social science, can make a significant difference in business success.

Budget Considerations in Implementing HR Strategies

Human resources is constantly challenged to do more with less. While we can complain about this reality, it holds true for our colleagues in finance, marketing, and IT (information technology), as well. In every organization where I have implemented a new HR strategy, it has worked by redirecting expense, not adding new expense.

Automation is usually the first place to start. HR forms and processes need to be moved online, and employee and manager self-service introduced. Employee questions and easy-to-resolve problems can be moved to a shared service center so HR employees can be free to address important business challenges.

HR leaders need to understand how to make a business case to receive approval from executives on technology investments. I have rarely failed to receive approval for significant HR investments because I could demonstrate real economic return in the short term or show how the investment was critical to support the business strategy.

The Key Challenge of the Future

The most significant challenge for HR leaders will continue to be talent management. Finding talented people, developing them, and providing tools to manage their performance will become even more important as demographic and economic changes challenge companies' ability to survive and grow.

HR is uniquely positioned to take charge of talent management. The place to start is to develop a deep understanding of the workforce. The list below summarizes the key questions that must be answered. By using the data gathered from the analysis, HR can facilitate the building of an integrated plan that includes talent assessment, the identification of high-potential employees, talent acquisition and on-boarding, and performance management:

- Is there a methodology in place to differentiate jobs according to their importance to the strategy?
- What are the key jobs that support the core components of the business strategy?
- What are the background competencies and expertise of the successful employees in these jobs?
- What are the turnover and growth rates of these key jobs?
- Is the recruitment and development infrastructure in place to meet future talent needs?

Summary

Human resources can make a significant contribution to organizational success. It starts with good planning and strategic thinking. Ours is a profession where the urgent often overwhelms the important. A well-thought-out strategy, an aligned structure, great HR talent, and the latest tools and concepts will make the difference and earn HR leaders a seat at the table.

John Daniel is the executive vice president of human resources for First Horizon Corporation. Before joining First Horizon, he was head of human resources at Regions Financial Corporation. He has served in senior human resources roles at Union Planters Bank, PNC Bank, and Mellon Bank Corporation.

Mr. Daniel grew up in Pittsburgh and earned his bachelor's degree in political science from the University of Pittsburgh. He moved his family to Germantown, Tennessee, in 2001 to work for Union Planters, which later became part of Regions. He and his wife have three sons.

The Power of HR Strategies to Change Corporate Culture

Karla Gochenour
Vice President, Human Resources
Woodmen of the World

ASPATORE

An Eye-Opening Introduction

In 2003, I switched companies, jumped industries, and entered a whole new world. The president of the organization told me his primary concern was succession planning. The organization was more than one hundred years old and had long-term leadership that was nearing retirement age. Turnover was rare. New blood and new ideas were even rarer. I spent a few months reviewing systems and learning the culture. One man summed it up when he told me, "You don't get invited to meetings until you've been here at least ten years, and it's another ten years before they'll let you talk." Recruiting, training and development, rewards and recognition, and corporate culture were so tightly intertwined that there was no way we could fix just one piece. We needed a comprehensive strategy.

Three months after my arrival, I sat down with the president and delivered my assessment: we needed a succession plan that would ensure business continuity and position the organization for success in the future. Unfortunately, the components that were needed to drive the plan were non-existent or so antiquated that it would be impossible to obtain the results we needed—performance management, compensation, and reward strategies, etc. It's to our president's great credit that he didn't show me the door right then. Instead, he gave me huge latitude to work with a talented internal team to rebuild the organization from the foundation. My team and I used a number of approaches to create a comprehensive strategy that would develop our existing talent, as well as retain and acquire new talent who were a good fit with our organization, all the while keeping our employees engaged.

Defining Core Competencies

As I looked at our leadership structure, I realized that it was probable that we could lose 50 percent to 70 percent of our leadership team to impending retirements. I had to devise an effective strategy for identifying and then developing internal talent to replace those leaders before they walked out the door.

We quickly identified strategic core competencies needed to ensure our future success. The identification of those competencies was a critical first step in the development of existing talent. Before we could name successors to our retiring leaders, we had to determine what our organization needed to be successful at to remain competitive in the marketplace. The competencies gave us something to measure our current talent against and to identify strengths and potential gaps in critical areas of our workforce.

Creating a Leadership Development Program

Once we identified what our company needed to excel at to remain competitive and profitable, we began a talent assessment process to locate employees who were most capable of filling our impending leadership vacuum. Employees who were the most skilled in our core competencies were targeted for an intense eighteen-month leadership development course to accelerate their learning to ensure they were prepared to assume expanded duties and roles when they became available.

Over the past three years, the majority of retiring leaders were replaced with employees from that development program. Between 70 percent and 80 percent of program participants have assumed a higher-level position, including several at the director and vice presidential level. We also began targeting middle-tier employees—those who would be ready for expanded duties in the next two to five years—by offering competency classes and other development opportunities, such as job shadowing, redeployment, and targeted development opportunities.

Developing the Right Internal Talent

We are committed to developing our internal talent. Having already addressed our top talent's development needs, we plan to focus on challenging our suitably placed employees. We need to keep those employees engaged and continuously improving. We plan to involve them much more in the development of newer employees who have been identified as having high potential to advance within the organization and assume expanded job duties over time.

Suitably placed, engaged employees have a great deal of valuable insight to offer to our new employees just joining the organization. We want to leverage their enthusiasm to reduce the learning curve for new employees and get them performing at their full capacity more quickly. That will lead to an increase in overall productivity, which feeds back into our big-picture business goals.

Transitioning Intellectual Capital

As boomers continue to leave the marketplace, we will have to keep our focus on transitioning intellectual capital to their successors. A wealth of information walks out the door when someone retires. We plan to capture that knowledge before it leaves.

We encourage our employees approaching retirement to work with their managers to identify successors and train them to assume their positions before they retire. Ideally, we want to have the successor in place for the last few months of each retiree's tenure. This helps ensure that knowledge transfer actually occurs and gets the successor operating at full capacity before the most knowledgeable resource for their position is no longer available.

Performance Management and Reward Programs

As I considered how to improve the overall productivity of our employees, I faced some hard truths. The first was that we weren't good at performance management. And second, our rewards and recognition didn't drive desired results. We had a deeply rooted culture of entitlement. For many of our employees, this was the only organization they had ever worked for, and the majority stayed until retirement because of our excellent benefits. Promotion and compensation based on tenure became an underlying assumption throughout our workforce.

Through repetitive companywide communication and training, we started to change the culture. We redesigned our entire performance appraisal process, tying compensation to performance, which in turn was connected to our competencies. Employees set goals with their managers and met quarterly (and in many cases monthly) to monitor progress. Raises and bonuses were based on achievement of goals. Individuals with less direct control over attainment of organizational goals had their compensation tied more to personal and department goals, while leadership found their compensation linked directly to the achievement of stated organizational goals.

A goal-driven performance appraisal process to which employees are held accountable allows poor performers to be identified and helps them improve their performance, find a more appropriate role that allows them to utilize their skills, or exit the organization. This also allowed us to start focusing on creating appropriate awards for our high performers. This change in philosophy allowed us to then shift our resources and offer incentive bonuses to every employee in the organization, regardless of management/responsibility level. This move achieved universal buy-in and helped us retain and reward the right talent.

Employee Involvement

As in any change initiative, employee involvement was critical. As we continued to shift the culture, it was crucial that we find ways to directly involve the employees in the process. They needed to feel a part of the change rather than feel something was just happening to them.

Let's be honest: the solutions to most business issues generally exist within the minds of our employees. They do the work, so they often know how to make it better. The challenge was taking time to speak directly with them and then really listening. Early on we involved our employees in the selection of competencies to help them embrace the changes we were instituting and more importantly because their input was invaluable. We were changing the way they'd be evaluated, developed, and compensated, and we needed their buy-in for it to run smoothly.

Compensation Strategies

Redeployment, creation of job families, and salary banding were incredibly helpful compensation strategies for my team as we restructured the way we paid our employees. We redeployed some of our most tenured employees into positions better suited for their strengths and skill sets. As a result, these employees, who had been disengaged, started enjoying their work more and producing better results.

Since our company had such a low attrition rate, the creation of job families was one critical way we could keep our talented employees engaged. Employees need to have something to reach for, and career paths with salary and duty distinctions provide motivation for employees to develop their skills and advance without leaving the company.

Finally, we assessed the salaries of our positions against those in our local market to ensure that our salaries were competitive. We also added salary bands to our positions to give employees room to navigate through their salary ranges, earning additional compensation commensurate with their performance without needing to make a traditional promotional move.

Employee Engagement

The final HR strategy focused strongly on employee engagement. Engaged employees deliver greater return on investment. They generate innovative products and service improvements and keep an organization one step ahead of its competitors.

Effective engagement strategies arise from candid employee feedback, so over the years, we have commissioned surveys to reveal what motivates our workforce. Supervisor successor training, self-development tracks, and position exploration are strategies that arose from survey results.

For a long time, we promoted the best doers, who don't always make the best managers. We developed a supervisor successor-training program to give those interested in management an opportunity to try supervising before they assume the role. Sessions expose participants to the different elements of supervisory work—administration, performance reviews, delivering constructive feedback, handling conflict, and understanding compliance and employment laws. The program confirms the desires of some and reveals a different career path for others. The bottom line is that we don't lose engaged employees who thought they wanted to be managers when an individual contributor role actually suits them better.

We ask all our managers to identify successors for their positions and develop those successors so that no position is left without an informed, skilled employee ready to assume it. Finally, by allowing employees to explore additional duties not normally part of their job descriptions, but in which they have interest, we are able to keep them challenged. Any position can continually be redefined; an employee's title, salary, and level of responsibility can change without their having to leave the company for a better opportunity.

Researching Strategies

Research is critical to the development and implementation of effective HR strategies. The most effective strategies consider a number of critical elements, such as best practices from successful companies, emerging technologies, and employee feedback, and are tied to business goals.

Making the most of those components requires thorough research. Thanks to the Internet, we have a world of data available to us at the click of a button. In the past we relied on networking contacts to share their own company's practices or data on a specific topic. That information is now housed in online databases that we can use to investigate and analyze critical information needed to make the best decision for the organizations we support.

Technology and HR

The speed of information has increased along with the technologies we use to equip our workforces. Many solutions are driven by technology; however, HR can prove its worth to an organization by proving that the best technology is useless in the hands of people who don't know how to use it.

In terms of HR applications, many great technology options exist, but they come at a cost. Purchase decisions have to be evaluated based on the value they return to your organization. I had to ask myself, "At what cost is process improvement justified?" With all the changes we were driving, I knew it was the perfect time to leverage our internal talent to develop creative solutions that improve efficiencies without incurring the cost of an all-inclusive software system.

Research was critical in determining which route I decided to take, not only with the purchase of new technology systems, but also with the implementation of all of our HR initiatives. Thorough analysis helped me determine my organization's true needs and find cost-effective solutions to meet those needs.

Managing Health Care Costs

In the next year, our company will continue to face the challenge of rising health care costs. In the past, we've offered varying plan designs to help employees and our organization manage rising health care expenses. We will continue to offer those flexible options when possible, along with a greater focus on various educational components.

We also need to help employees become better consumers by realizing that they have options when it comes to their health care. They choose which doctors they see, which routes of treatment they take, and which health facilities they visit. Health care is a business like anything else, and the more we help our employees understand that, the less they will yield unquestioningly to physician advice, and the more they will exercise wisdom in their decision-making regarding health care for themselves and their families.

Having a strong partnership with your health care provider is critical when dealing with these challenges. For example, our provider offered generic prescriptions at no cost to plan participants for three months. It was a strategy on the provider's part to reduce prescription drug costs by educating consumers about the value of generic drugs. We made sure our employees knew about it and used it. As a result, it had an impact on future decisions to use generic drugs when they are available and a favorable impact on cost.

Implementing Wellness Programs

We are also implementing a significant push toward wellness programs within our company. There was only so much altering we could do to our plan design. At some point we had to commit to changing our employees' mindsets and behaviors. We started the pursuit of that goal with an annual wellness survey to help employees explore areas of strength and weakness in their daily habits.

The first year, we offered an incentive payment to their medical flexible spending accounts to participate in the survey. The response was positive, and we were able to use the feedback, not only to educate our employees, but also to devise new strategies aimed at improving the overall wellness of our workforce.

For example, response overwhelmingly indicated that employees wanted access to an on-site fitness facility. Their voices, along with the requisite research proving the cost savings over time to our company in terms of reduced benefits expenses, convinced our senior leadership that the fitness facility was a worthwhile investment. A year later we had an on-site, staffed fitness facility and an increasing number of employees taking advantage of it. Healthier employees translate into lower benefits expenses. As our workforce grows healthier and makes wise choices regarding their health care, such as visiting doctors instead of urgent care facilities whenever possible, our costs to insure them decrease. Our employees feel the benefits not only in their own enjoyment of life, but also by seeing lower plan cost increases from year to year.

Teaching Personal Finance Management

As a financial services company, another strategy we plan to undertake during the coming year is to educate our employees about financial wellness. People get into financial situations that cause them stress in relationships, their health, and their jobs, which can result in poor performance and affect the organization negatively. We must help people be as knowledgeable as they can be about their financial situation. This includes education about wise spending habits and appropriate saving for retirement and college. Since our sales agents are professionals at helping consumers do this, instead of paying someone to come in and offer this information to our workforce, we are using our sales agents to offer financial wellness classes to our employees.

Measuring Success

As we implement new strategies, we will continually evaluate all of them. We have a set of wellness metrics in place to measure the programs we are rolling out to improve our employees' physical and financial wellness. For example, a noticeable decrease in claims and leaves of absence will tell us that we have implemented the right strategies. We also have an annual tool in place to measure employee engagement and to reveal areas with opportunities for improvement.

The Year Ahead

Over the next year, a struggling economy and the continued exodus of baby boomers from the marketplace will have an impact on our HR strategies. These challenges will force us all to become even more creative than we have been in the past with strategy development and execution. Rising gas and food prices will continue to strain our employees.

Offering flexible workplace options, such as telecommuting for more employees whose attitudes and positions are well-suited for it, can help ease this stress and keep our employees from seeking employment outside of our company. We will need to develop customized solutions for our employees. One-size-fits-all plans won't help us retain productive workforces. We need to do what makes sense, as well as get creative about the implementation of sensible initiatives.

The Power of Successful HR Strategies

Human resources should not operate independently of its organization. Effective strategies are tied to organizational goals and have the buy-in of leadership before they are implemented. All successful HR strategies attract, retain, and engage talented employees. These strategies arise from research that incorporates employee feedback. Strategies that produce desirable results further cement the role of human resources, not as an administrative support role, but as a critical partner in the quest for profitability and a productive workforce.

Karla Gochenour is vice president, human resources, at Woodmen of the World—one of the largest fraternal benefit societies in the United States. Her primary focus is overseeing employee relations, workforce planning, recruiting, group benefits, talent management, and training.

Prior to joining Woodmen of the World in 2003, Ms. Gochenour was an independent consultant for a Fortune 500 company, assisting the company in establishing a merger and acquisition process. Prior to that, she spent more than seventeen years at First Data Resources, primarily in human resources. Her last position was vice president, human resources, specializing in employee relations, mergers and acquisitions, and crisis management.

As a seasoned advocate for managing human capital, Ms. Gochenour has a passion for all of the dynamics of human resources, including change management and the development of tomorrow's leaders. She also has an uncanny ability to perform as a business analyst. Her ability to maintain a seat at the executive level ensures her contributions are exemplary. She has attended and successfully completed numerous executive-level leadership courses, including the Center for Creative Leadership, and the Leadership Development program through the Leadership Research Institute.

In the first phase of her career, Ms. Gochenour attended Iowa Western Community College and graduated as a surgical technician. She currently serves on the board of directors of the Institute for Career Advancement Needs (ICAN), St. Peter Claver Cristo Rey High School, and is a member of the Society for Human Resource Management. She also continues to proudly serve her community as a Woodmen of the World, Alpha Lodge member, a vital part of volunteer activities and disaster relief within the community and the country.

ASPATORE